Dominating Money

Tapping into God's Supernatural Economy

Dr. J. Victor and Catherine B. Eagan

Workplace Wisdom®Publishing, L.L.C.
Orchard Lake, Michigan

Other Books Authored by the Eagans Include:

How to Discover Your Purpose in 10 Days
God's Path to a Full and Satisfied Life

How to Discover Your Purpose in 10 Days
Prayers & Daily Journal

How to Discover Your Purpose in 10 Days
Self-Assessment Workbook

Dominating Business
How to Prosper on Your Job

Anointed for Work
Using the Tools from Sunday to Succeed on Monday

How to Determine Your Motivational Gift
Learn How God Wired You

The Character of Success
26 Characteristics of Highly Successful People

The Word @ Work, Volume I
Scriptures for the Workplace

The Word @ Work, Volume II
Scriptures for the Workplace

Upcoming Books include:

Godly Leadership in the Workplace

The Road to the Wealthy Place
Dominating Money in Business

Terminating Conflict in the Workplace
God's Solutions to Resolving Conflict Permanently on the Job

All titles are available on-line at www.eaganbooks.com.
Also available: CDs and DVDs.
For more information, e-mail us at info@eaganbooks.com
Or call 1-877-EAGANS1 (324-2671).

Dominating Money
Tapping into God's Supernatural Economy

To order this title by mail in the United States of America, please include the price of $35.00 per book along with $6.95 postage and handling. Increased postage is required for additional books ordered. Send to Workplace Wisdom Publishing.

ISBN 0-9678889-3-X

Unless otherwise identified, all Scripture quotations in this publication are taken from the following books:

- Holy Bible, King James Version (KJV)
- New King James Version (NKJ) Copyright ©1979, 1980, 1982 by Thomas Nelson, Inc., Used by permission. All rights reserved.
- New International Version (NIV) © 1973, 1978, 1984 International Bible Society. Used by permission of Zondervan Bible Publishers. All rights reserved.
- Amplified Bible (AMP) Scripture taken from The Amplified Bible, Old Testament copyright © 1965, 1987 by the Zondervan Corporation. The Amplified New Testament copyright © 1958, 1987 by The Lockman Foundation. Used by permission.

Mailing Address:
Workplace Wisdom® Publishing
17600 W. 12 Mile Road, Suite 4
Southfield, Michigan 48076

Printed in the United States of America
For Worldwide Distribution

Workplace Wisdom Institute

ENDORSEMENTS

Dr. J. Victor and Minister Catherine Eagan are seasoned Bible teachers who do an excellent job of presenting both the natural and supernatural side of Financial Prosperity. Their material is simply outstanding and a must for all who truly want to prosper God's way.

Rev. Keith A. Butler, II, Pastor
Faith Christian Center
Smyrna, Georgia

The Eagan's have done a masterful job of presenting powerful truths from God's Word on finances. We urge everyone to not only read this book but to also put into operation the principles outlined. These practical, scriptural insights will transform your life!

Pastor & Mrs. Thomas G. Wilson
Word of Faith Christian Center,
Kentwood, Michigan

We are eternally grateful to Dr. and Mrs. J. Victor Eagan for teaching the Financial Seminar on "Dominating Money." My congregation will never be the same since they have grabbed hold of these valuable teachings. I want to challenge all Pastors to have this seminar taught to your congregation. It will change their lives forever!

Pastor Michael L. Tucker
Faith Christian Center,
Savannah, Georgia

I have used the financial biblical principles and have incorporated good stewardship, faithfulness, and trustworthiness into my life and now, I am being elevated and rewarded in many ways that one year ago were unimaginable. Minister Catherine Eagan spoke into my life on March 12, 2002, and all of what was spoken has come to pass. So much so, that I went to Dr. Victor Eagan and he spoke wisdom and clarity into my situation and life. As I obeyed his direction, the Lord blessed me and has given me great success within six weeks.

ENDORSEMENTS, continued

I have opened myself up to bigger horizons outside of this city and state and I have been offered a million dollar opportunity in another state. I have become free to speak about my weaknesses and indebtedness and now I am becoming totally debt free after over twenty years in the medical profession. My wife took the course in 2001; it has changed both of our lives. We don't go to Word of Faith, but are in leadership at Holy Ghost Cathedral. The principles and anointing on the Eagans' have definitely helped to secure my mission and my calling as a gastroenterologist.

Lee C. Laney Jr., M.D.
St. John Health System
Gastroenterology

I truly thank God the Father, for your obedience to His perfect plan in your lives. You are a constant resource of God's wisdom to me. All the Kingdom Business Association courses have been a great blessing to me, but this has been the most pivotal. Before this course, I was in financial bondage crying to get out. Finances were always a topic of intense fellowship in our home. I was a woman with a wallet afire with strong fear of numbers.

Through the Holy Spirit upon your lives, I'm aware of how much God loves me. My husband and I can now have a conversation about finances, without fears, tears, and frustration. We are of one mind when we speak of passing a good name to our children. God has also spoken to my heart that as I write down the vision for our financial deliverance He will bring it to pass. Matthew 5:18 says, "Blessed are the pure in heart for they shall see God." I believe that because of your motives to see my classmates and I whole financially, you both shall see God manifested in every area of your iives.

Tanya N. Hall
Student

TABLE OF CONTENTS

DEDICATION

This book is dedicated to every Christian who believes that they are called to manage wealth for the Kingdom of God to the glory of God.

ACKNOWLEDGEMENTS

God has blessed us with so many outstanding people who helped us and allowed this manual to become a reality. We are eternally grateful to our spiritual leaders, our parents, and a host of outstanding individuals.

We want to first acknowledge and thank God who has given us revelation knowledge in the area of business and finance and has magnificently blessed us as a demonstration of His desires for His children.

As a couple working together in business and ministry and loving each other deeply and more deeply each day, we must acknowledge and thank each other and God for a joyful, anointed, inspired, and growth experience working together.

Special thanks to our mothers, Mrs. Louise Eagan and Mrs. Adele Cartey, who trained us up in the way in which we should go, inspired us through their lifestyles, prayed for us without ceasing, taught us unselfishly, helped us financially, and blessed us beyond measure.

We thank our pastor; Bishop Keith A. Butler, and his lovely wife, Minister Deborah L. Butler, who over the past 18 years have developed us spiritually, mentored us, and encouraged us to grow in the gifts and call on our lives and thus be in the center of God's perfect will.

We thank Kenneth Copeland Ministries for the use of their estate planning materials Jewell Datcher, our Executive Assistant; Gina Rozier, for Technical Support; Denise Stinson, our Literary Agent; Jim Friedman, Attorney; Gary Fenderson, Joan Gist, Stacey Hanks, Kelsey Schwartz, Lauren Doyle Davis, and Geralda Sellers for helping produce the material for distribution.

Workplace Wisdom Institute

FOREWORD

The Church of the Lord Jesus Christ has been redeemed! Galatians 3:13 states, "Christ hath redeemed us from the curse of the law, being made a curse for us." (KJV) We have been redeemed from poverty, sickness, and separation from God through the Blood of Jesus Christ! Therefore, we don't have to be poor, sick, or separated from God. That's what the Word of God says and believers ought to receive the Word and act on it.

It is God's perfect will for the Church to prosper more, specifically to prosper financially. This is confirmed in God's Word. III John 2 states, "Beloved, I wish above all things that thou mayest prosper and be in health, even as thy soul prospereth." (KJV) The word *"as"* is an adjective that denotes "at the same time," according to Noah Webster's Dictionary of 1828. Moreover, the Church is called to prosper financially and *at the same time* enrich its mind, will, and emotional understanding of money.

In order for financial prosperity to occur, certain conditions must be met:

- You must get God's Word on the matter.
- You must act in line with the Word of God.
- You must sow seed to meet your needs.
- You must learn fundamental financial principles.

A seed will meet any need! Seedtime and harvest is a principle that God's Word says shall not cease (Genesis 8:22). Sowing seed is the catalyst that moves the hand of God to supernaturally work on your behalf.

Dominating Money, Tapping into God's Supernatural Economy is an important book for every member of the Body of Christ. While it brings revelation from the Word of God in many areas of finance and money, it centers on the practical aspects of managing and dominating money

from a biblical perspective. It provides the ammunition for your soul to prosper. Victor and Catherine teach the principles of God on finance and money by giving practical steps for debt reduction, credit restoration, cash flow management, wealth building, investments, estate planning, insurance, and taxes.

The Eagans are teaching ministry gifts. They are anointed, trained, and very capable to teach and preach in the areas of finance and business. They are called to the Body of Christ, and God has used them to change the lives of thousands both nationally and internationally.

At Word of Faith International Christian Center - Workplace Wisdom Institute, by the power of God, they have been empowering people of all ages and denominations to pursue wealth to the Glory of God.

For over 18 years, I have been honored to be the pastor of the Eagans. They have served faithfully and are fulfilling their purpose and destiny in the will of God for their lives.

The manual, *Dominating Money, Tapping into God's Supernatural Economy* is biblically sound and has been an outstanding blessing to the Word of Faith family of churches and to churches across the country and around the world.

Bishop Keith A. Butler

Pastor and Founder
Word of Faith International Christian Center
Southfield, Michigan

Workplace Wisdom Institute

PREFACE

INTEGRATING FAITH INTO THE WORKPLACE

This manual introduces the following seven objectives or paradigm shifts essential for Christians in the workplace:

- Teach individuals that one of man's primary reasons for being created by God is to work, which is the stewardship, dominion, and management of the earth and its resources for the Kingdom of God.
- Expose and destroy the myth that leads individuals to believe their work life should be segmented and independent from their relationship with God.
- Aid and assist every individual in determining, understanding, and fulfilling their God-given purpose in the workplace.
- Assist individuals in understanding that every Christian is in full time ministry and that how they perform in the workplace is important and vital to the plans and purposes of God.
- Teach individuals that the proper implementation of God's wisdom in the workplace is essential for the effective operation and management of their work environment.
- Teach, train, and equip individuals to properly apply their faith in God at work, thereby positively enhancing their work ethic, integrity, and character.
- Assist Christian workers in understanding that their placement in the work environment affords God an opportunity to evangelize in the workplace through them.

Workplace Wisdom Institute

INTRODUCTION

God needs His people to be wealthy. He has desires, which He wants to accomplish in the earth through His people. God has called Christians or followers of the Anointed One and His anointing to be wealthy. God's desires for us are far beyond what we could ever think of or ask for. As such, He has made every provision for us to be wealthy, healthy, and wise. With wealth from God, the healing power of the Anointing, and the wisdom of God, every Christian should be dominating money, whether you earn $20,000 or $1,000,000.

The Word of God empowers Christians to gain wealth, maintain it, bless others with it, enjoy it, and pass it inter-generationally. However, many are struggling financially and have yet to see the manifested turnaround in their cash flow. This manual is designed to teach every Christian how to dominate money and have an economic sphere of influence on the earth to the glory of God. ***You cannot go to the wealthy place unless you first learn how to dominate money.***

As children of God, we should be financial dominators. Our impact must be worldwide and demonstrated through the mastery of money in every sphere of influence. Christians have relegated the domination of finances, money, and business to the non-Christian. This has resulted in the perverted use of money, business, and possessions.

Every Christian needs to have a revelation that God wants His people in charge of managing the earth on His behalf. We are His stewards on the earth. For this reason, God's first spiritual instructions to man were to be fruitful, multiply, fill the earth, subdue it, and to dominate it (Genesis 1:26, 28).

Genesis 1:26: Then God said, "Let Us make man in Our own image, according to Our likeness, let them have dominion, over the fish of the sea, over the birds of the air, and over the cattle, over all the earth, and over every creeping thing that creeps on the earth." (NKJ)

Workplace Wisdom Institute

INTRODUCTION, continued

Genesis 1:28 Then God blessed them, and God said to them "Be fruitful and multiply; fill the earth and subdue it and have dominion...

Adam was empowered before he was physically formed in the earth. It was not until Genesis 2:7 that man was formed by God. Similarly, before we were ever born God spoke and foreordained wealth and money domination into the lives of His children. As a result, the Word of God says "God takes pleasure in the prosperity of His servant."

Psalm 35:27

27 Let them shout for joy, and be glad, that favour my righteous cause: yea, let them say continually, Let the LORD be magnified, who has pleasure in the prosperity of his servant. (NKJ)

God enjoys when His people are righteous and wealthy, godly leaders!

Many in the Body of Christ who are believing God for increase in their finances, know the Word of God, and are fully persuaded that God has called them to be wealthy. Yet, they are still financially strapped to meet basic needs. Whenever the issue of money comes up they are pressed on every side.

Then, there are others who have realized economic gain but know in their hearts that where God wants them to be is far greater. While everyone would call them a financial success they feel incomplete and not fully developed financially. In many cases, this is because, they are not using money to glorify God but themselves – their motives are wrong.

For Christians to dominate money for the Kingdom of God, they need to have a thorough understanding of God's principles and practical applications as they relate to the effective management and stewardship of money.

These include:

- Properly Utilizing God's Purpose for Money
- Knowing How to Tap into God's economy
- God's Principles of Financial Ruin and Increase
- Eliminating Debt
- Repairing Your Credit
- Understanding Insurance and Risk Management
- Understanding Investment Planning and How to Grow Assets
- Estate Planning – The Wealth Transfer

Dominating Money deals with very sensitive financial issues in a practical way to assist and propel the Body of Christ on its road to the wealthy place.

It is our prayer that every person who reads this manual implements its plans and strategies. The Word of God implores us, "But be ye doers of the word, and not hearers only, deceiving your own selves." James 1:22. (KJV)

If you believe that you are called of God to grow financially, we believe that there is an anointing on the book and the materials included for God to work through any situation for you to dominate money to the glory of God.

We are praying for financial increase upon every person who reads our material.

May God richly bless you,

Dr. J. Victor and Catherine B. Eagan

NOTES

Workplace Wisdom Institute

Keys to Dominating Money for the Kingdom of God

Workplace Wisdom Institute

Keys to Dominating Money for the Kingdom of God

The Lord gave His children authority and dominion over the entire earth. This dominion extends to money and finances.

Genesis 1:26

26 Then God said, "Let Us make man in Our image, according to Our likeness; let them have dominion over the fish of the sea, over the birds of the air, and over the cattle, over all the earth and over every creeping thing that creeps on the earth." (NKJ)

Psalm 8:4-6

4 What is man that You are mindful of him, and the son of man that You visit him?
5 For You have made him a little lower than the angels, and You have crowned him with glory and honor.
6 You have made him to have dominion over the works of Your hands; you have put all things under his feet, (NKJ)

Christians should be the most effective people and businesspeople when it comes to managing money and finances in the entire world. God can give insight to His children that the world cannot access. He has all wisdom, knowledge, and ability. And He desires to transfer this knowledge and ability to us for His glory and honor.

2 Peter 1:3

3 as His divine power has given to us all things that pertain to life and godliness, through the knowledge of Him who called us by glory and virtue, (NKJ)

When we choose not to fully access the anointing to prosper and the financial promises of God, it produces financial lack in our lives.

The following keys are necessary for the Christian to dominate money and finances for the Kingdom of God.

Keys to Dominating Money for the Kingdom of God

Notes

Number One (1)

Understanding and properly utilizing God's purpose and design for money

In order for the Christian to dominate money for the Kingdom of God, God's perspective towards money must be maintained. Money must be utilized according to God's purpose and design.

God never intended money to be used for security, for controling others, for selfish gain, for looking and feeling important, for spending only as your heart desires, or for promoting wickedness. He created money for glorifying Himself, for establishing the Kingdom of God, for provision, for providing direction, for serving others, for promoting righteousness, and for enjoyment.

When a Christian misuses money or does not fully understand its intended purpose, it leads to financial difficulties. However, when money is utilized in its proper context, it sets the stage for financial increase.

Number Two (2)

Effectively establishing the Kingdom of God in the earth through tithes and offerings

Deuteronomy 8:18

18 "And you shall remember the LORD your God, for it is He who gives you power to get wealth, that He may establish His covenant which He swore to your fathers, as it is this day. (NKJ)

God desires that His Kingdom increase throughout the earth. Money and finances are vital to the growth and maintainance of the Kingdom of God on the earth.

Notes

Number Two (2)

Effectively establishing the Kingdom of God in the earth through tithes and offerings, continued

God has preordained that 10% of all money that is stewarded by the Christian be automatically earmarked to go to the local church. Donations and offerings above the tithe are also to be given to the local church and other Christian ministries.

When tithes and offerings are not properly appropriated to the local church and other Christian ministries, God counts the Christian as stealing and operating in wickedness. God will not bless the Christian who robs Him financially.

Malachi 3:8-9

8 "Will a man rob God? Yet you have robbed Me! But you say, 'In what way have we robbed You?' In tithes and offerings.
9 You are cursed with a curse, for you have robbed Me, even this whole nation.
(NKJ)

However, when a Christian gives tithes and sows offerings into the local church and other Christian ministries, it sets the stage for supernatural harvest.

Number Three (3)

Faithfully stewarding and managing money and possessions for the Kingdom of God

The faithful stewardship of money and possessions begins with the understanding that we own nothing but manage everything for the Kingdom of God.

1 Corinthians 4:2

2 Moreover it is required in stewards that one be found faithful. (NKJ)

Notes

Faithful stewardship includes:

- Proper budgeting

- Eliminating debt

- Faithfully handling money and possessions

- Maintaining excellent care of the money and possessions under your control

- Not attempting to manage more than you are currently prepared to handle

- Maximizing or increasing the money or possessions under your control
- Proper insurance planning
- Proper estate planning

Number Four (4)

Developing and operating in godly character

The development and maintenance of godly character is absolutely essential to the effective stewardship and domination of money and possessions for the Kingdom of God.

2 Peter 1:5-8

5 But also for this very reason, giving all diligence,
add to your faith virtue, to virtue knowledge,
6 to knowledge self-control, to self-control perseverance, to perseverance godliness,
7 to godliness brotherly kindness, and to brotherly
kindness love.
8 For if these things are yours and abound, you will
be neither barren nor unfruitful in the knowledge
of our Lord Jesus Christ. (NKJ)

Keys to Dominating Money for the Kingdom of God

Notes

Godly character qualities include:

Creativity vs. Under Achievement

Diligence vs. Slothfulness

Thoroughness vs. Incompleteness

Dependability vs. Inconsistency

Patience vs. Restlessness

Flexibility vs. Resistance

Availability vs. Self-Centeredness

Endurance vs. Giving Up

Orderliness vs. Disorganization

Initiative vs. Unresponsiveness

Responsibility vs. Unreliability

Decisiveness vs. Double Mindedness

Resourcefulness vs. Wastefulness

Punctuality vs. Tardiness

Excellence vs. Mediocrity

Wisdom vs. Natural Inclinations

Faith vs. Presumption

Alertness vs. Unawareness

Determination vs. Faint-heartedness

Boldness vs. Fearfulness

Discernment vs. Judgment

Enthusiasm vs. Apathy

Self-Control vs. Self-Indulgence

Security vs. Anxiety

Keys to Dominating Money for the Kingdom of God

Discretion vs. Simple Mindedness

Respectfulness vs. Disrespect

Hospitality vs. Loneliness

Generosity vs. Stinginess

Joyfulness vs. Self-Pity

Humility vs. Pride

Loyalty vs. Unfaithfulness

Attentiveness vs. Unconcern

Sensitivity vs. Callousness

Justice vs. Fairness

Compassion vs. Indifference

Gentleness vs. Harshness

Deference vs. Rudeness

Meekness vs. Anger

Truthfulness vs. Deception

Obedience vs. Willfulness

Sincerity vs. Hypocrisy

Virtue vs. Impurity

Forgiveness vs. Rejection

Persuasiveness vs. Contentiousness

Thriftiness vs. Extravagance

Contentment vs. Covetousness

Tolerance vs. Prejudice

Cautiousness vs. Rashness

Notes

Notes

Number Four (4)

Developing and operating in godly character, continued

The Christian who desires to dominate money absolutely must learn and develop the character qualities of diligence, faithfulness, and responsibility. Diligent people dominate money; whereas, lazy and slothful people become poor and are dominated by others.

Proverbs 10:4

4 Lazy hands make a man poor, but diligent hands bring wealth. (NIV)

Number Five (5)

Maintaining righteousness, morality, and integrity

The Bible has a lot to say about moral behavior and how it affects the Christian financially. It commands us to absolutely avoid wickedness such as adultery, fornication, homosexuality, perversion, lying, stealing, cheating, substance abuse, etc. The consequences of ungodly behavior are death, destruction, and financial ruin.

1 Corinthians 6:9-10

9 Do you not know that the unrighteous will not inherit the kingdom of God? Do not be deceived. Neither fornicators, nor idolaters, nor adulterers, nor homosexuals, nor sodomites,
10 nor thieves, nor covetous, nor drunkards, nor revilers, nor extortioners will inherit the kingdom of God. (NKJ)

However, when Christians decide to walk in righteousness, holiness, and integrity in their financial dealings, they invite God to actively participate in their finances; thereby, positively affecting their financial situations.

Notes

Ecclesiastes 2:26

26 For God gives wisdom and knowledge and joy to a man who is good in His sight; but to the sinner He gives the work of gathering and collecting, that he may give to him who is good before God. This also is vanity and grasping for the wind. (NKJ)

Number Six (6)

Understanding and operating in God's ordained purpose for your life

There is a supernatural connection between wealth and a person operating in their God-ordained purpose. God foreordained and predestinated who we would be and our path in life. This path contains God's greatest anointing for your life and allows you to accomplish God's will for your life.

Ephesians 2:10

10 For we are God's (own) handiwork (His workmanship); recreated in Christ Jesus, (born anew) that we may do those good works which God predestined (planned beforehand) for us (taking paths which He prepared ahead of time), that we should walk in them (living the good life which He prearranged and made ready for us to live). (AMP)

Moreover, the Christian who knows and operates in their purpose will be a blessing to others, have their individual needs met, and walk in God's financial best for their life.

Number Seven (7)

Developing excellence and a high level of quality in your work output

Christians who develop and operate in excellence in their workplace set up the spiritual and natural environment to attract money and finances to themselves.

Notes

Number Seven (7)

Developing excellence and the high level of quality in your work output, continued

When a person is dissatisfied with a product, service, or the work output of an individual or business, they begin to seek a product and service somewhere else. This decreases the cash or wealth transfer.

However, when people are pleased with a product, service, or a person's work output, it encourages them to purchase more product or service, thereby maintaining or increasing cash or wealth transfer.

Therefore, operating in excellence in the workplace increases the potential of dominating money for the Kingdom of God.

Number Eight (8)

Developing financial intelligence

Christians who dominate financially for the Kingdom of God not only have spiritual intelligence, they also have financial intelligence. Financial intelligence includes understanding the natural principles of money and finance.

These include thoroughly understanding:

- analyzing financial statements, balance sheets, and income statements
- analyzing investment deals and transactions
- analyzing investment portfolios (stocks, bonds, real estate, mutual funds, etc.

- Tax implications of financial and business transactions
- Financial and business planning
- Succession planning
- Financial implications of leadership and management
- Business growth and development
- How to get excellent advisors. (i.e., lawyers, accountant, broker, financial planner, bankers)
- Hidden costs of business transactions (i.e. fees, insurance, advisors, casualty, etc.)

Notes

Number Nine (9)
Maintaining excellent health

3 John 1:2

2 Beloved, I pray that you may prosper in all things and be in health, just as your soul prospers. (NKJ)

- Maintaining excellent health allows the individual to live a full, productive life and not die prematurely, resulting in financial loss.
- Maintaining excellent health allows a person to operate at the top of their efficiency in the workplace and as a money manager.

Notes

Number Nine (9)

Maintaining excellent health, continued

- Sickness, disease, and fatigue diminish the ability of an individual to create wealth and manage existing money and possessions effectively. They are often a drain on money and resources.
- Regular physical examinations
- Proper nutrition
- Eating healthy
- Daily exercise
- Proper rest and relaxation
- Proper confession and application of the Word of God and prayer in healing

Number Ten (10)

Fully integrating the Bible, prayer and your relationship with God into all of your financial affairs

God desires that the Bible, prayer and your relationship with Him be fully integrated into every aspect of your life, especially your finances.

Integrating the Bible, prayer, and operating on biblical principles in your financial affairs ensures that the will of God will be accomplished in your finances. God's anointing on your finances brings financial success.

2 Timothy 3:16,17

16 Every Scripture is God-breathed (given by His
inspiration) and profitable for instruction, for
reproof and conviction of sin for correction of
error and discipline in obedience, (and) for
training in righteousness (in holy living, in confor-
mity to God's will in thought, purpose, and action),
17 So that the man of God may be complete
and proficient, well fitted and thoroughly
equipped for every good work. (AMP)

Ephesians 6:18

18 praying always with all prayer and supplication in the Spirit, being watchful to this end with all perseverance and supplication for all the saints—(NKJ)

1Thessalonians 5:17

17 pray without ceasing, (NKJ)

Being a Money Dominator

Jesus Christ is my Lord, not money.

My life does not revolve around the pursuit, accumulation, and maintenance of money.

I control money. Money or the lack of it does not control me.

I can effectively manage the money and possessions that are under my stewardship to the glory of God.

I am a faithful tither to my local church, and I give significant offerings to my local church and other Christian ministries.

I fully understand God's purposes for money and am committed to accomplishing His purpose for money and finance in the earth.

Notes

Being a Money Dominator, continued

I am generous. I am a financial blessing to many people.

I live a life of personal and financial integrity. I do not involve myself in wickedness such as lying, cheating, stealing, substance abuse, or sexual immorality. I am an example of Christian character.

I know how to plan financially. I can prepare a budget very well, and I follow it. I live below my income.

I am not controlled or rattled with debt. I have eliminated my debt, and I am free to achieve God's will and purpose in my life financially.

I have effectively accessed and prepared my risk management by properly insuring my risk areas such as cars, homes, health, and liability.

I have properly prepared for the inter-generational wealth transfer of the finances that I steward. I have a current will and have planned the orderly transfer of my estate through a meaningful estate plan.

I spend less money than I earn. I have a six months supply saved in an emergency fund and have long-term savings effectively placed in the appropriate investment vehicles.

The Role of Money

Workplace Wisdom Institute

The Role of Money

Money is powerful!

Some have said that it is not love that makes the world go around, but money - cash flow! It is undisputable that money influences almost every decision that a person has made in the past, is making in the present, and will make in the future. Money is a determinant.

John D. Rockefeller, Sr., was known as The First Billionaire and The World's Richest Man at the turn of the 20th century. When questioned about his money, he avidly stated "God gave me my money." (Chernow, Titan, 1997, p.54) What was it about Rockefeller and God that caused Rockefeller to be a dominator? Perhaps he understood something as a Christian that has evaded many 21st century Christians when it comes to money. "Rockefeller always adverted to his own adherence to the doctrine of stewardship - the notion of the wealthy man as a mere instrument of God, a temporary trustee of His money, who devoted it to good causes. 'It seemed as if I was favored and got increase because the Lord knew that I was going to turn it around and give it back.'" (Chernow, Titan, 1997, p.57.)

God is concerned about money, and has given His people specific instructions regarding it. In the Word of God, there are approximately 500 verses of scripture on prayer, fewer than 500 on faith, but more than 2,350 verses on how to handle money.

Many Christians are missing the financial blessing of God because they don't understand the role of money from God's perspective. This chapter discusses:

- The Influence of Money
- What is Money?
- The Quest for Ownership and Possessions

The Role of Money

- Personal Stewardship
- If 10% is for Tithes, What About the Remaining 90%?

The Role of Money is designed to bring clarity, understanding, and great increase into the hands of believers to the glory of God.

Notes

The Influence of Money

Money determines your ethics and morality.

Money influences all of your relationships.

- Choice of marital partner
- Marital success
- Decisions about family planning
- Family relationships
- Friendships
- Enemies
- Job relationships
- Church relationships

Money is a Determinant

Notes

Money influences:

- Career choices
- Business and management decisions
- Nation building
- Political and governmental decisions
- Quality of life
- Church issues
- Social issues
- Educational issues
- General decision making

Conclusion Point
Money influences every aspect of life.

Ecclesiastes 10:19b
19 ... but money answers everything. (NKJ)

Notes

What Does the Bible Say About Money?

There are approximately 500 verses on prayer, fewer than 500 on faith, but more than 2,350 verses on how to handle money.

God is very concerned about how we handle money.

Jesus said that there are two "masters" or controlling forces on the planet: God and mammon.

God Almighty, Jehovah, clearly wants us to serve Him only!

Matthew 6:24

24 No one can serve two masters; for either he will hate the one and love the other, or else he will be loyal to the one and despise the other. You cannot serve God and mammon. (NKJ)

Exodus 20:3-6

3 You shall have no other gods before Me.
4 You shall not make for yourself a carved image, or any likeness of anything that is in heaven above, or that is in the earth beneath, or that is in the water under the earth;
5 you shall not bow down to them nor serve them. For I, the Lord your God, am a jealous God, visiting the iniquity of the fathers on the children to the third and fourth generations of those who hate Me,
6 but showing mercy to thousands, to those who love Me and keep My commandments. (NKJ)

Definition of an Idol:

Any object of ardent or excessive devotion that you place trust in and reliance on to determine the course and path of your future.
(Random House Dictionary of the English Language, Random House, 2nd Ed., New York, 1984, page 951.)

Characteristics of Idolatry

- Worship
- Fear and reverence
- Security
- Trust and reliance
- Direction

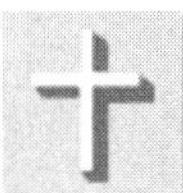

1 Corinthians 10:12-14

12 Therefore let him who thinks he stands take heed lest he fall.
13 No temptation has overtaken you except such as is common to man; but God is faithful, who will not allow you to be tempted beyond what you are able, but with the temptation will also make the way of escape, that you may be able to bear it.
14 Therefore, my beloved, flee from idolatry. (NKJ)

Conclusion Point
Excessive devotion to money is a form of idolatry.

Notes

Workplace Wisdom Institute

Notes

Money Talks

- I can make you successful.
- I can make you happy.
- I will take care of you — you can trust in me.
- I will secure your future.
- I will make your relationships good.
- I will bring you anything your heart desires.

1 Timothy 6:10

10 For the love of money is a root of all kinds of evil. Some people, eager for money, have wandered from the faith and pierced themselves with many griefs. (NIV)

Ecclesiastes 5:10-11

10 Whoever loves money never has money
enough; whoever loves wealth is never satisfied
with his income. This too is meaningless.
11 As goods increase, so do those who consume
them. And what benefit are they to the owner
except to feast his eyes on them? (NIV)

What is Money?

Notes

Money is a medium.

Definition of medium:

A medium is a middle state; an intervening thing through which a force acts; any means, agency, etc.; a means of communication to reach a general public; it's a vehicle, a tool.

(Random House Dictionary of the English Language, Random House, 2nd Ed., New York, 1984, page 1195.)

- Money is neutral.
- Money is neither moral nor immoral.
- Money has no response.
- Money is neither positive nor negative.

Money is time, resources, talent, and ability in a transferable form.

What is Mammon?

Mammon is not just money.

Mammon = possessions

Greek definition of mammon:

Mammonas: a common Aramaic word for riches and possessions. (Strong's Exhaustive Concordance of the Bible, Thomas Nelson Publishers, Nashville, 1990, page 46.)

Matthew 6:24

24 No one can serve two masters; for either he will hate the one and love the other, or else he will be loyal to the one and despise the other. You cannot serve God and mammon. (NKJ)

Notes

What Possessions Represent Modern Day Mammon?

- Houses
- Cars
- Jewelry
- Jobs
- Businesses

Conclusion Point
People are more concerned with the power, possessions, and influence that money can obtain than they are with the money itself.

Conclusion Point
The quest for money is really a quest for possessions.

Luke 12:15

15 And He said to them, "Take heed and beware of covetousness, for one's life does not consist in the abundance of the things he possesses." (NKJ)

Ecclesiastes 5:10-11

10 He who loves silver will not be satisfied with silver; nor he who loves abundance, with increase. This also is vanity.
11 When goods increase, they increase who eat them; so what profit have the owners except to see them with their eyes? (NKJ)

Why is Mammon So Powerful?

Is our inordinate (excessive) desire for possessions an abomination to God?

The quest for ownership and possessions strikes at the heart of God.

Psalm 24:1

1 The earth is the Lord's, and all its fullness, the world and those who dwell therein. (NKJ)

Psalm 50:10-12

10 For every beast of the forest is Mine, and the cattle on a thousand hills.
11 I know all the birds of the mountains, and the wild beasts of the field are Mine.
12 If I were hungry, I would not tell you; for the world is Mine, and all its fullness. (NKJ)

Haggai 2:8

8 'The silver is Mine, and the gold is Mine,' says the LORD of hosts. (NKJ)

Psalm 89:11

11 The heavens are Yours, the earth also is Yours; the world and all its fullness, You have founded them. (NKJ)

Psalm 100:3

3 Know that the Lord, He is God; it is He who has made us, and not we ourselves; we are His people and the sheep of His pasture. (NKJ)

1 Corinthians 10:26

26 for "the earth is the Lord's, and all its fullness." (NKJ)

Fundamental Truth
The world and everything in the world, including man, all belong to God.

Notes

Notes

Why is Mammon So Powerful?

continued

Our inordinate desire to possess things is a perversion of stewardship.

Definition of a steward:

A steward is a person who manages another's property or financial affairs, who administers anything as an agent for others.

(Random House Dictionary of the English Language, Random House, 2nd, New York, 1987, page 1868.)

We don't own anything; we are managers or stewards for God.

God wants us to manage for Him.

Psalm 8:6

6 You have made him to have dominion over the works of Your hands; you have put all things under his feet, (NKJ)

Jesus was tempted — Satan tried to get Jesus to steward for him.

Notes

Luke 4:5-8

5 Then the devil, taking Him up on a high mountain, showed Him all the kingdoms of the world in
a moment of time.
6 And the devil said to Him, "All this authority I will
give You, and their glory; for this has been delivered to me, and I give it to whomever I wish.
7 "Therefore, if You will worship before me, all will
be Yours."
8 And Jesus answered and said to him, "Get
behind Me, Satan! For it is written, 'You shall worship the Lord your God, and Him only you shall
serve.'" (NKJ)

God wants to steward the world for Himself. And, Satan wants to steward for himself. They both want to use you.

Who are you allowing to use your body to steward the world? Whose kingdom are you stewarding for?

Notes

Why is Mammon So Powerful?
continued

Our desire for possessions is a quest for self-reliance — independence from God.

Deuteronomy 8:17-18

17 then you say in your heart, My power and the might of my hand have gained me this wealth.
18 And you shall remember the Lord your God, for it is He who gives you power to get wealth, that He may establish His covenant which He swore to your fathers, as it is this day. (NKJ)

We should rely on God rather than our possessions.

Proverbs 3:5

5 Trust in the Lord with all your heart, and lean not on your own understanding; (NKJ)

1 Timothy 6:17-19

17 Command those who are rich in this present age not to be haughty, nor to trust in uncertain riches but in the living God, who gives us richly all things to enjoy.
18 Let them do good, that they be rich in good works, ready to give, willing to share,
19 storing up for themselves a good foundation for the time to come, that they may lay hold on eternal life. (NKJ)

If you put your trust and reliance on possessions, you are out of the will of God.

The Rich, Young Ruler

Notes

Luke 18:18-23

18 Now a certain ruler asked Him, saying, "Good
Teacher, what shall I do to inherit eternal life?"
19 So Jesus said to him, "Why do you call Me
good? No one is good but One, that is, God.
20 "You know the commandments: 'Do not
commit adultery,' 'Do not murder,' 'Do not steal,'
'Do not bear false witness,' 'Honor your father
and your mother.'"
21 And he said, "All these I have kept from my
youth."
22 So when Jesus heard these things, He said to
him, "You still lack one thing. Sell all that you have
and distribute to the poor, and you will have treasure in heaven; and come, follow Me."
23 But when he heard this, he became very
sorrowful, for he was very rich. (NKJ)

Jesus Christ is not Lord over all of a person's life unless He is also Lord over their finances and possessions.

Let's be God-oriented rather than possession-oriented.

Notes

Zacchaeus

Luke 19:1-10

1 Then Jesus entered and passed through Jeri-
cho.
2 Now behold, there was a man named
Zacchaeus who was a chief tax collector, and he
was rich.
3 And he sought to see who Jesus was, but could
not because of the crowd, for he was of short
stature.
4 So he ran ahead and climbed up into a syc-
amore tree to see Him, for He was going to pass
that way.
5 And when Jesus came to the place, He looked
up and saw him, and said to him, "Zacchaeus,
make haste and come down, for today I must
stay at your house."
6 So he made haste and came down, and received Him joyfully.
7 But when they saw it, they all complained,
saying, "He has gone to be a guest with a man
who is a sinner."
8 Then Zacchaeus stood and said to the Lord,
"Look, Lord, I give half of my goods to the poor;
and if I have taken anything from anyone by false
accusation, I restore fourfold."
9 And Jesus said to him, "Today salvation has
come to this house, because he also is a son of
Abraham;
10 "for the Son of Man has come to seek and to
save that which was lost." (NKJ)

An intimate encounter with God will change your relationship with, and perspective toward, possessions and people.

Personal Stewardship of Finances and Resources

Notes

One of the reasons Christians fall into financial difficulty is because their thinking on financial issues is improper.

Romans 12:2

2 Do not be conformed to this world (this age), (fashioned after and adapted to its external, superficial customs), but be transformed (changed) by the (entire) renewal of your mind (by its new ideas and its new attitude), so that you may prove (for yourselves) what is the good and acceptable and perfect will of God, *even* the thing which is good and acceptable and perfect (in His sight for you). (AMP)

If you are attempting to approach money from a worldly perspective, you will never be able to achieve God's results.

If you want God's results, you must renew your mind (think as God thinks) and operate on His principles.

Notes

Personal Stewardship of Finances and Resources, continued

Stewardship Has Eternal Consequences

Definition of a steward:

A steward is a person who manages another's property or financial affairs, who administers anything as an agent for others.

(Random House Dictionary of the English Language, Random House, 2nd, New York, 1987, page 1868.)

The Greek definition of *oikonomos* is three words – manage, overseer, supervisor

A steward is the supreme authority under his master and has full responsibility for all his master's possessions and household affairs.

God owns everything, and He wants Christians to manage everything in the world to His glory.

Psalm 8:6

6 You have made him to have dominion over the works of Your hands; You have put all things under his feet, (NKJ)

Paradigm Shift

We own nothing, but manage everything for God.

"If silver and gold are things evil in themselves, then those who keep away from them deserve to be praised. But if they are good creatures of God, which we can use both for the needs of our neighbor and for the glory of God, is not a person silly, yes, even unthankful to God, if he refrains from them as if they were evil?"

Martin Luther

Progressive Revelation of Financial Stewardship

Notes

Stage 1:

We own everything (100%). We have complete control over our own financial decisions. We are accountable only to ourselves.

Stage 2:

God owns 10% (tithe). We own 90%.

Stage 3:

God owns everything (100%). We are temporary managers or stewards for Him.

Wisdom Point

Everything belongs to God, and we are temporary managers or stewards. When we die, we immediately transfer the right to manage temporal possessions to someone else.

Fundamental Principle

What happens with the 10% tithe and the other 90% that you personally manage is important in the plans and purposes of God.

Many Christians believe that they do not have enough to manage, yet they ignore the reality of the significant amount of money which flows through their hands.

Notes

Personal Stewardship of Finances and Resources, continued

How do we properly steward for God?

1. We have to be in relationship with God through Jesus Christ.

John 3:16

16 For God so loved the world that He gave His only begotten Son, that whoever believes in Him should not perish but have everlasting life. (NKJ)

1 John 1:9

9 If we confess our sins, He is faithful and just to forgive us our sins and to cleanse us from all unrighteousness. (NKJ)

2. We must be in communication with God.

   a. Prayer

Philippians 4:6

6 Be anxious for nothing, but in everything by prayer and supplication, with thanksgiving, let your requests be made known to God; (NKJ)

   b. Pray without ceasing.

1 Thessalonians 5:17

17 pray without ceasing, (NKJ)

Praying without ceasing is living our lives as a continual attitude of prayer in constant communication with God, the Father. Two-way communication is:

1. Talking to God

2. Hearing from God

Wisdom Point
The ability to hear from God precisely is extremely important in order to be an effective steward of money and possessions, for the Kingdom of God.

Notes

3. We must be led by the Spirit of God.

Romans 8:14
14 For as many as are led by the Spirit of God, these are sons of God. (NKJ)

John 5:30
30 I can of Myself do nothing. As I hear, I judge; and My judgment is righteous, because I do not seek My own will but the will of the Father who sent Me. (NKJ)

Most people make the majority of their decisions based on:

- Intellect (what I think I should do)
- Emotions (what I feel I should do)
- Demonic activity (ungodly behavior manifested in other people)

4. We must obey God.

   a. Obedience

1 Samuel 15:22
22 Then Samuel said: "Has the Lord as great delight in burnt offerings and sacrifices, as in obeying the voice of the Lord? Behold, to obey is better than sacrifice, and to heed than the fat of rams." (NKJ)

Notes

Personal Stewardship of Finances and Resources, continued

Two ways to get rich:

- God's way
- Satan's way

Money is a magnifier. Money magnifies what is really on the inside of a person. The more money someone controls, the more their behavior is exaggerated. This is why a person needs to be right with God (holy, exercising Christian character) before they accumulate large amounts of money.

5. We must be Faithful.

1 Corinthians 4:2

2 Moreover it is required in stewards that one be found faithful. (NKJ)

Definition of Faithful:

Strict or thorough in the performance of duty. True to one's word, promises, vows, etc., reliable, trusted. (Random House Dictionary of the English Language, Random House, 2nd, New York, 1987, page 693.)

We are to be faithful to what we are entrusted with.

The Faithful Steward

Notes

Matthew 25:14-26

14 For the kingdom of heaven is like a man traveling to a far country, who called his own servants
and delivered his goods to them.
15 And to one he gave five talents, to another
two, and to another one, to each according to
his own ability; and immediately he went on a
journey.
16 Then he who had received the five talents
went and traded with them, and made another
five talents.
17 And likewise he who had received two gained
two more also.
18 But he who had received one went and dug
in the ground, and hid his lord's money.
19 After a long time the lord of those servants
came and settled accounts with them.
20 So he who had received five talents came
and brought five other talents, saying, 'Lord, you
delivered to me five talents; look, I have gained
five more talents besides them.'
21 His lord said to him, 'Well done, good and
faithful servant; you were faithful over a few
things, I will make you ruler over many things.
Enter into the joy of your lord.'
22 He also who had received two talents came
and said, 'Lord, you delivered to me two talents;
look, I have gained two more talents besides
them.'
23 His lord said to him, 'Well done, good and
faithful servant; you have been faithful over a few
things, I will make you ruler over many things.
Enter into the joy of your lord.'
24 Then he who had received the one talent
came and said, 'Lord, I knew you to be a hard
man, reaping where you have not sown, and
gathering where you have not scattered seed.
25 And I was afraid, and went and hid your talent
in the ground. Look, there you have what is
yours.'
26 But his lord answered and said to him, 'You
wicked and lazy servant, you knew that I reap
where I have not sown, and gather where I have
not scattered seed. (NKJ)

Notes

Personal Stewardship of Finances and Resources, continued

Matthew 25:27-30

27 So you ought to have deposited my money with the bankers, and at my coming I would have received back my own with interest.
28 Therefore take the talent from him, and give it to him who has ten talents.
29 For to everyone who has, more will be given, and he will have abundance; but from him who does not have, even what he has will be taken away.
30 And cast the unprofitable servant into the outer darkness. There will be weeping and gnashing of teeth. (NKJ)

1. God is the owner of everything and has the right to recover and hold us accountable for what He has given us to manage.
2. God will entrust to us that which is within our own ability to manage and not beyond.
3. God thoroughly disapproves of slothfulness on our part and expects us to multiply the assets, not just maintain them.

Notice: The Master did not multiply the assets for the individual who was unfaithful. Also, the steward did the work to multiply what was given.

Faithfulness with little things is important to God.

The Lord rewards faithfulness regardless of the amount over which we are entrusted.

The Lord does not, however, reward the "lotto mentality": "something for nothing".

The Role of Money

Luke 16:10

10 He who is faithful in what is least is faithful also in much; and he who is unjust in what is least is unjust also in much. (NKJ)

"Small things are small things but faithfulness with a small thing is a big thing." Hudson Taylor

Faithfulness with another's possessions determines how much you are entrusted with in your future.

Luke 16:12

12 And if you have not been faithful in what is another man's, who will give you what is your own? (NKJ)

Romans 14:12

12 So then each of us shall give account of himself to God. (NKJ)

2 Corinthians 5:9-10

9 Therefore we make it our aim, whether present or absent, to be well pleasing to Him.
10 For we must all appear before the judgment seat of Christ, that each one may receive the things done in the body, according to what he has done, whether good or bad. (NKJ)

The Lord holds us accountable for how we handle money.

Matthew 25:19

19 After a long time the lord of those servants came and settled accounts with them. (NKJ)

Notes

Workplace Wisdom Institute

Notes

Personal Stewardship of Finances and Resources, continued

Wisdom Point
When we acknowledge God's ownership, every spending decision becomes a spiritual decision with eternal consequences.

God requires us to be faithful in handling 100% of the money entrusted to us.

- The church has primarily concentrated on teaching how to manage the tithes and offerings, which is approximately 10-15% of our income.
- We traditionally learn how to handle the remaining 85-90% from the world's perspective, not the Lord's perspective.

As a result of not being equipped to handle money biblically, many Christians have wrong attitudes toward money and possessions.

This causes them to make incorrect and ungodly financial decisions.

Hosea 4:6

6 My people are destroyed for lack of knowledge. Because you have rejected knowledge, I also will reject you from being priest for Me; because you have forgotten the law of your God, I also will forget your children. (NKJ)

Ignorance or disobedience to scriptural financial principles frequently causes money problems.

"Jesus Christ said more about money than about any other single thing because, when it comes to a man's real nature, money is of first importance. Money is an exact index to a man's true character. All through Scripture there is an intimate correlation between the development of a man's character and how he handles his money."

Richard Halverson

Matthew 6:21

21 For where your treasure is, there your heart will be also. (NKJ)

The use of money and possessions is an indicator of a person's eternal values. How we handle and spend money reveals to which kingdom we have alligence. When we waste money, purchase ungodly items or support ungodly people or causes, we are demonstrating our allegiance to the kindom of darkness. However, when we effectively steward money and possessions for God by giving to Christian causes, using money for noble purposes, and assisting those in need, we are pledging our allegiance to the Kingdom of God.

Wisdom Point

If you see a person's checkbook, you have seen their heart.

Notes

Module
Study Questions

1. Who trusted in their possessions more than they trusted in God?
   A) Zacchaeus
   B) The rich, young ruler
   C) Both

2. Any object of ardent or excessive devotion that you place trust in and reliance on to determine the course or path of your future:
   A) God
   B) Worship
   C) Idol
   D) None of the above

3. "Whoever loves money never has money enough," is found in:
   A) Ecclesiastes 10:19
   B) Ecclesiastes 5:11
   C) Ecclesiastes 5:10
   D) Haggai 2:8

4. _______ is time, resources, talent, and ability in a transferable form.
   A) Mammon
   B) Medium
   C) Possessions
   D) Money

5. The quest for money is really a quest for possessions.
   A) True
   B) False

6. Everything in the world, except man, belongs to God.
   A) True
   B) False

7. In Matthew 6:24, Jesus said that there were two gods or controlling forces on the planet: God and satan.
   A) True
   B) False

The Role of Money

8. Money influences:
   A) Quality of life
   B) Church issues
   C) All of your relationships
   D) Political and government decisions
   E) All of the above

9. Excessive devotion to money is a form of:
   A) Idolatry
   B) Worship
   C) Security
   D) Trust and reliance

10. There are approximately how many verses in the Bible on how to handle money?
    A) 500
    B) 1,200
    C) 2,000
    D) 2,350

11. "But money answers everything," is found in:
    A) Ecclesiastes 6:5
    B) Ecclesiastes 10:19
    C) Matthew 6:24
    D) Colossians 3:5

12. Money influences every aspect of life.
    A) True
    B) False

13. "For the love of money is a root of all kinds of evil," is found in:
    A) 1 Timothy 6:10
    B) 2 Timothy 5:2
    C) Colossians 3:5
    D) Romans 4:12

Module
Study Questions, continued

14. "The earth is the Lord's and all its fullness," is found in:
    A) Psalm 100:3
    B) Psalm 50:10
    C) 1 Corinthians 10:26
    D) Luke 12:15

15. "Some people eager for money have wandered from the faith and pierced themselves with many griefs," is found in:
    A) 1 Timothy 6:10
    B) 2 Timothy 5:2
    C) Colossians 3:5
    D) Romans 4:12

16. Money determines your ethics and morality.
    A) True
    B) False

17. Money equals mammon.
    A) True
    B) False

18. "No one can serve two masters...you cannot serve God and mammon," is found in:
    A) Ecclesiastes 6:5
    B) Ecclesiastes 10:19
    C) Matthew 6:24
    D) Colossians 3:5

19. An inordinate desire to possess things is a perversion of ________.
    A) Stewardship
    B) Worship
    C) Security
    D) Kingdom Work

The Role of Money

20. In what Bible passage did satan try to get Jesus to steward the world for him?
    A) Luke 18:18-23
    B) Luke 19:1-10
    C) Matthew 5:25-34
    D) Luke 4:5-8

21. The account of the rich, young ruler is found in:
    A) Luke 18:18-23
    B) Luke 19:1-10
    C) Matthew 5:25-34
    D) Luke 4:5-8

22. The story of Zacchaeus is found in:
    A) Luke 18:18-23
    B) Luke 19:1-10
    C) Matthew 5:25-34
    D) Luke 4:5-8

23. "Command those who are rich in this present age not to be haughty, nor trust in uncertain riches but in the living God, who richly gives us all things to enjoy," is found in:
    A) Deuteronomy 8:17
    B) 1 Timothy 6:17
    C) Colossians 3:5
    D) 1 Timothy 6:10

24. Our desire for possessions is really a quest for:
    A) Security
    B) Money
    C) Independence from God
    D) None of the above

25. "The silver is mine, and the gold is mine, says the Lord of Hosts," is found in:
    A) Psalm 24:1
    B) Psalm 50:10
    C) Psalm 89:11
    D) Haggai 2:8

Module
Study Questions, continued

26. A person who manages another's property or financial affairs, who administers anything as an agent for others.
    A) Supervisor
    B) Steward
    C) Kingdom worker

27. The Lord rewards faithfulness regardless of the amount to which a person is entrusted.
    A) True
    B) False

28. Faithfulness with another's possessions determines how much you are entrusted with.
    A) True
    B) False

29. The Lord will not hold us accountable for how we handle money.
    A) True
    B) False

30. God will only hold us accountable for how we manage our tithes and offerings. The rest of the money we can manage according to our own purpose.
    A) True
    B) False

31. There is an intimate correlation between the development of a man's character and how he handles money.
    A) True
    B) False

32. Ignorance or disobedience to scriptural financial principles frequently causes money problems.
    A) True
    B) False

33. Every spending decision is a spiritual decision with eternal consequences.
    A) True
    B) False

God's Purposes for Money

God's Purposes for Money

God designed everything with and for a purpose. When people use an item for the purpose that God intended, success can be achieved. However, if someone misuses an item or does not follow the intended purpose for the item, difficulty and failure occur. God never intended money to be used for security, to control others, for selfish gain, to look and feel important, to spend to your heart's desire, or promote wickedness. He created money to glorify Himself, to establish the Kingdom of God, for provision, to provide direction, to serve others, to promote righteousness, and for enjoyment.

This chapter addresses the improper and proper uses of money from God's perspective.

Improper Uses of Money

Notes

1. Money should not be used as security.

Proverbs 11:28

28 He who trusts in his riches will fall, but the righteous will flourish like foliage. (NKJ)

Job 31:24,25,28

24 "If I have made gold my hope, or said to fine gold, 'You are my confidence';
25 If I have rejoiced because my wealth was great, and because my hand had gained much;
28 This also would be an iniquity worthy of judgment, for I would have denied God who is above. (NKJ)

Proverbs 3:5

5 Trust in the LORD with all your heart, and lean not on your own understanding; (NKJ)

1 Timothy 6:17

17 Command those who are rich in this present age not to be haughty, nor to trust in uncertain riches but in the living God, who gives us richly all things to enjoy. (NKJ)

Conclusion Point

Money or the acquisition of money should never be used as security or to create independence from God. Our trust and reliance should always be on God.

Notes

Improper uses of money, continued

2. Money should not be used to control others.

Zechariah 7:9-10

9 "Thus says the LORD of hosts: 'Execute true justice, show mercy and compassion everyone to his brother.
10 Do not oppress the widow or the fatherless, the alien or the poor. Let none of you plan evil in his heart against his brother.' (NKJ)

Ezekiel 18:5-9

5 "Suppose there is a righteous man who does what is just and right.
6 He does not eat at the mountain shrines or look to the idols of the house of Israel. He does not defile his neighbor's wife or lie with a woman during her period.
7 He does not oppress anyone, but returns what he took in pledge for a loan. He does not commit robbery but gives his food to the hungry and provides clothing for the naked.
8 He does not lend at usury or take excessive interest. He withholds his hand from doing wrong and judges fairly between man and man.
9 He follows my decrees and faithfully keeps my laws. That man is righteous; he will surely live, declares the Sovereign LORD. (NIV)

Conclusion Point

Money should never be used to exert power or influence over others. It should never be used to put others in bondage. Money should be a blessing in the lives of other people.

Notes

3. **Money should not be used for selfish gain.**

1 Timothy 6:17-19

17 Command those who are rich in this present age not to be haughty, nor to trust in uncertain riches but in the living God, who gives us richly all things to enjoy.
18 Let them do good, that they be rich in good works, ready to give, willing to share,
19 storing up for themselves a good foundation for the time to come, that they may lay hold on eternal life. (NKJ)

Philippians 2:3-4

3 Do nothing out of selfish ambition or vain conceit, but in humility consider others better than yourselves. (NIV)
4 Each of you should look not only to your own interests, but also to the interests of others (NKJ)

Conclusion Point

Money was not designed by God to be used primarily for yourself. God desires that His people be a financial conduit by which He can bless others.

"Real Christians are givers to others first. They give time, energy, and money."
Bishop Keith A. Butler, Sr.

4. **Money should not be used to look and feel important.**

Jeremiah 9:23-24

23 Thus says the LORD: "Let not the wise man glory in his wisdom, let not the mighty man glory in his might, nor let the rich man glory in his riches;
24 But let him who glories glory in this, that he understands and knows Me, that I am the LORD, exercising lovingkindness, judgment, and righteousness in the earth. For in these I delight," says the LORD. (NKJ)

Notes

Improper uses of money, continued

4. Money should not be used to look and feel important.

Psalm 138:6

6 Though the LORD is on high, yet He regards the lowly; but the proud He knows from afar. (NKJ)

Proverbs 16:18

18 Pride goes before destruction, and a haughty spirit before a fall. (NKJ)

Proverbs 21:24

24 The proud and arrogant man—"Mocker" is his name; he behaves with overweening pride. (NIV)

Proverbs 25:27

27 It is not good to eat too much honey, nor is it honorable to seek one's own honor. (NIV)

Proverbs 29:23

23 A man's pride will bring him low, but the humble in spirit will retain honor. (NKJ)

Jeremiah 13:15

15 Hear and pay attention, do not be arrogant, for the LORD has spoken. (NIV)

2 Corinthians 10:12

12 We do not dare to classify or compare ourselves with some who commend themselves. When they measure themselves by themselves and compare themselves with themselves, they are not wise. (NIV)

Conclusion Point

Money is not to be used to exalt oneself over others.

Notes

5. **Money should not be used to spend only as your heart's desires.**

Haggai 2:8

8 `The silver is mine and the gold is mine,' declares the LORD Almighty. (NIV)

Conclusion Point

All money, riches, and possessions belong to God. We are only temporary stewards. The faithful steward manages as the true owner (God) desires. So, you must pray and seek God's direction before spending money.

6. **Money should not be hoarded for yourself.**

Luke 12:15-21

15 And He said to them, "Take heed and beware of covetousness, for one's life does not consist in the abundance of the things he possesses."
16 Then He spoke a parable to them, saying: "The ground of a certain rich man yielded plentifully.
17 "And he thought within himself, saying, `What shall I do, since I have no room to store my crops?'
18 "So he said, `I will do this: I will pull down my barns and build greater, and there I will store all my crops and my goods.
19 `And I will say to my soul, "Soul, you have many goods laid up for many years; take your ease; eat, drink, and be merry."'
20 "But God said to him, `Fool! This night your soul will be required of you; then whose will those things be which you have provided?'
21 "So is he who lays up treasure for himself, and is not rich toward God." (NKJ)

Workplace Wisdom Institute

Notes

Improper uses of money, continued

Conclusion Point
Money can be saved or collected in moderation. However, it should never be hoarded. It all belongs to God and He must have the freedom to use it as He wishes.

Wisdom Point
Financial trouble generally arises when an individual misuses money and does not follow God's purpose and design.

7. Money should never be used to promote wickedness, evil behaviors, or desires.

1Thessalonians 5:22

22 Abstain from every form of evil. (NKJ)

Proverbs 4:14-15

14 Do not enter the path of the wicked, and do
not walk in the way of evil.
15 Avoid it, do not travel on it; turn away from it
and pass on. (NKJ)

Proverbs 8:13

13 The fear of the LORD is to hate evil; pride and arrogance and the evil way and the perverse mouth I hate. (NKJ)

Proverbs 14:16

16 A wise man fears the LORD and shuns evil, but a fool is hotheaded and reckless. (NIV)

1 Peter 3:10-11

10 For "He who would love life and see good
days, let him refrain his tongue from evil, and his
lips from speaking deceit.
11 Let him turn away from evil and do good; let
him seek peace and pursue it. (NKJ)

Conclusion Point
Money should never be used to promote wickedness or evil behavior in any form or fashion. God desires that money be used to promote righteousness and godly behavior.

Notes

Reasons for financial difficulty:

A. Individual misuses God's purpose or design for money.

B. Individual makes unwise financial decisions.

C. Individual does not fully understand or utilize God's purpose and potential for their life.

D. Individual is involved in immoral or ungodly behaviors.

E. Individual is struck by calamity or disaster and is financially unprepared.

Notes

God's Purpose and Design for Money

1. **Money should be used to glorify God.**

1 Corinthians 10:31

31 So whether you eat or drink or whatever you do, do it all for the glory of God. (NIV)

Conclusion Point

God should be glorified in every single action performed. Therefore, the use of money should bring glory and honor to God.

2. **Money should be used to establish the Kingdom of God in the earth.**

Deuteronomy 8:18

18 "And you shall remember the LORD your God, for it is He who gives you power to get wealth, that He may establish His covenant which He swore to your fathers, as it is this day. (NKJ)

2 Peter 3:9

9 The Lord is not slack concerning His promise, as some count slackness, but is longsuffering toward us, not willing that any should perish but that all should come to repentance. (NKJ)

Conclusion Point

God desires that every person enter into the saving knowledge of the Lord Jesus Christ. He also wants the Kingdom of God to expand throughout the earth.

Conclusion Point

The Kingdom of God is also established when churches, communities, businesses, and individuals capture a sphere of society and bring it under the Lordship of Jesus Christ.

3. **Money should be used for provision.**

Notes

Psalm 37:25

25 I have been young, and now am old; yet I have not seen the righteous forsaken, nor his descendants begging bread. (NKJ)

Psalm 23:1

1 The LORD is my shepherd; I shall not want. (KJV)

Philippians 4:19

19 And my God shall supply all your need according to His riches in glory by Christ Jesus. (NKJ)

Conclusion Point

Money should be utilized to provide for the needs of families, businesses and communities.

4. **Money should be used to provide direction.**

Isaiah 48:17

17 Thus says the LORD, your Redeemer, the Holy One of Israel: "I am the LORD your God, who teaches you to profit, who leads you by the way you should go. (NKJ)

Psalm 32:8

8 I will instruct you and teach you in the way you should go; I will counsel you and watch over you. (NIV)

Psalm 37:23

23 The steps of a good man are ordered by the LORD, and He delights in his way. (NKJ)

Notes

God's Purpose and Design for Money,
continued

Proverbs 3:5-6

5 Trust in the LORD with all your heart, and lean not on your own understanding;
6 In all your ways acknowledge Him, and He shall direct your paths. (NKJ)

Conclusion Point

God will use money or the lack of it to provide supernatural direction in the life of the believer.

5. **Money should be used to promote righteousness and godly behavior.**

Titus 3:8

8 This is a trustworthy saying. And I want you to stress these things, so that those who have trusted in God may be careful to devote themselves to doing what is good. These things are excellent and profitable for everyone. (NIV)

Hebrews 13:16

16 But do not forget to do good and to share, for with such sacrifices God is well pleased. (NKJ)

Galatians 6:10

10 Therefore, as we have opportunity, let us do good to all, especially to those who are of the household of faith. (NKJ)

3 John 1:11

11 Beloved, do not imitate what is evil, but what is good. He who does good is of God, but he who does evil has not seen God. (NKJ)

6. Money should be used to serve others who are in need.

Notes

Matthew 20:26-28

26 "Yet it shall not be so among you; but whoever desires to become great among you, let him
be your servant.
27 "And whoever desires to be first among you,
let him be your slave—
28 "just as the Son of Man did not come to be
served, but to serve, and to give His life a ransom
for many." (NKJ)

Philippians 2:4

4 Let each of you look out not only for his own interests, but also for the interests of others. (NKJ)

Proverbs 19:17

17 He who is kind to the poor lends to the LORD, and he will reward him for what he has done. (NIV)

Proverbs 28:27

27 He who gives to the poor will not lack, but he who hides his eyes will have many curses. (NKJ)

Proverbs 11:24-25

24 One man gives freely, yet gains even more;
another withholds unduly, but comes to poverty.
25 A generous man will prosper; he who refreshes
others will himself be refreshed.
(NIV)

1John 3:17-18

17 But whoever has this world's goods, and sees
his brother in need, and shuts up his heart from
him, how does the love of God abide in him?
18 My little children, let us not love in word or in
tongue, but in deed and in truth. (NKJ)

Notes

God's Purpose and Design for Money, continued

Conclusion Point
Money should be used to be a blessing in the lives of other people. God desires that we be generous in helping to meet the needs of others.

7. Money can be used for enjoyment.

1 Timothy 6:17

17 Charge them that are rich in this world, that they be not highminded, nor trust in uncertain riches, but in the living God, who giveth us richly all things to enjoy; (KJV)

Conclusion Point
God has provided riches and possessions for the enjoyment of the believer.

Note: Be cautious. Satan attempts to entice people to become unbalanced and spend too much time and energy on enjoying life, rather than on enjoying life while accomplishing the will of God at the same time.

Tapping Into God's Economy

Tapping Into God's Economy

God's economy operates based upon principles. The definition of a principle is "a fundamental, primary or general law or truth from which others are derived, a standard or test for measuring." (Random House Dictionary of the English Language, Random House, 2nd Ed., New York, 1984, page 1539.)

An example of a fundamental law is the law of universal gravitation. The law of gravitation states that any two masses attract each other with a force equal to a constant (constant of gravitation) multiplied by the product of the two masses and divided by the square of the distance between them. Now, you may not understand this law or the scientific formula, but if you jump out of a window, you will experience the attraction and the force!

Man may invent ways to defy gravity and other such laws, but man will never defy the Laws of God that are outlined in *Genesis 8: 22 "While the earth remaineth, seedtime and harvest, and cold and heat, and summer and winter, and day and night shall not cease." (KJV)*

Since the beginning, farmers have learned that from seed planted in good soil, watered over time, a harvest can be reaped. There are parts of this process that are inexplicable, and often times we take the process for granted. Yet, if the principles required to cause a harvest to grow are not followed, it does not matter how much seed was planted. There will be no harvest. Droughts during the farming season have been known to destroy an entire crop or cause the harvest to be small or underdeveloped. No water, no harvest.

Many people experience these consequences in their finances. They either don't understand the principles and fall flat on their financial faces, or they don't take the practical and natural steps to ensure their harvest, resulting in a money shortage or drought. Even in a disaster, there are ways to rebound. If proper planning occurs by understanding the Financial Laws of the Kingdom of God, you can survive.

Tapping Into God's Economy

This chapter, "Tapping into God's Economy," is devoted to furthering a believer's understanding of spiritual and natural principles for financial increase. It includes:

- Giving and Receiving
- Purpose - The Missing Link to Wealth
- Seedtime and Harvest
- Tithes and offerings
- Using the principles of God always causes us to triumph

Workplace Wisdom Institute

Notes

Giving and Receiving

Giving and receiving are two of the most powerful principles outlined in the Bible.

Luke 6:38

38 "Give, and it will be given to you: good measure, pressed down, shaken together, and running over will be put into your bosom. For with the same measure that you use, it will be measured back to you." (NKJ)

2 Corinthians 9:6-10

6 But this I say: He who sows sparingly will also reap sparingly, and he who sows bountifully will also reap bountifully.
7 So let each one give as he purposes in his heart, not grudgingly or of necessity; for God loves a cheerful giver.
8 And God is able to make all grace abound toward you, that you, always having all sufficiency in all things, may have an abundance for every good work.
9 As it is written: "He has dispersed abroad, He has given to the poor; His righteousness endures forever."
10 Now may He who supplies seed to the sower, and bread for food, supply and multiply the seed you have sown and increase the fruits of your righteousness, (NKJ)

Proverbs 11:25

25 The generous soul will be made rich, and he who waters will also be watered himself. (NKJ)

Tapping Into God's Economy

God is concerned about His people gaining and maintaining a financially dominant position on the earth. We must understand the importance of this to the Father. It is an inheritance given based upon God's promise to Abraham's seed and central to why Jesus came – to redeem us from the curse of poverty.

From the beginning of the Bible in Genesis, to its end in Revelation, God has commanded His people to rule and reign in this life on the earth. He does not set limits on any aspect of rulership or in any discipline.

We are commanded in Genesis 1:28 to:

a) Be fruitful - to increase, grow, and bring forth.

b) Multiply - abundance, to be full of, heap up.

c) Subdue - to conquer, force, and bring into subjugation.

d) Replenish - to be full in wide application, satisfy, and to have wholly.

e) Have dominion - to reign, to rule, to take.

Genesis 1:28

Then God blessed them, and God said to them, "Be fruitful and multiply; fill the earth and subdue it; have dominion over the fish of the sea, over the birds of the air, and over every living thing that moves on the earth." (NKJ)

(Hebrew definitions are taken from Strong's Concordance of the Bible, Thomas Nelson Publishers, Nashville, 1990, pages 96, 109, 54, 66, and 107.)

Notes

Giving and Receiving, continued

These are instructions, capabilities, attributes and qualities that God has **given** us. If we dare to **receive God's impartations** and walk in them in the area of finance, there is no limit to the scope of domination.

The Word of God says, "He has given us all things to enjoy." The apostle Paul told Timothy, in the New Testament, "Charge them that are rich in this world, that they be not high-minded, nor trust in uncertain riches, but in the living God, who giveth us richly all things to enjoy" (1Timothy 6:17). Spiritually, we must be ever mindful that God has given us riches to enjoy, with responsibility.

In order to dominate financially, you must have a ***revelation*** that God has **given** us the ability to be wealthy and has empowered us to be wealthy (Deuteronomy 8:18), but it all begins with the knowledge that **God gave**.

Given the massive ability that God has given us, it should be without a blink of the eye that we give God the tithe and the offering, at a minimum. Further, if we really understood the power that is within us through Christ Jesus and the Holy Spirit, the path which leads to accomplishing wealth would be clear.

We are made in the likeness and image of God, so we have the propensity to be givers and receivers. If we expect to receive financially from God, we must give into the Kingdom of God. The more we give, the greater the return – God created the risk-reward investment scenario. It's called faith and reward. Hebrews 11:6 states, "But without faith it is impossible to please him: for he that cometh to God

must believe that he is, and that he is a rewarder of them that diligently seek him."(KJV)

Notes

Are you asking God for ways He wants you to give? Are you synchronized with God in the areas which He wants you to receive? Open yourself up to the majesty of the King of Glory and see how good God really is financially. He always wants to do " . . . exceeding, abundantly above all that we can think or ask according to the power that works in us." (Ephesians 3:20)

Scriptural Implications

- God honors generosity.
- Giving is a form of expressing thanksgiving to God for what He has already given to you.
- If you are faithful in giving and receiving, you open the door for your needs to be met and an abundance besides.

Practical Implications

Practical Application

"Just do it."

Don't "give to get;" give from the heart.

Giving and receiving are equally important — be balanced.

Notes

Giving and Receiving, continued

Give To:

- Your local church (tithes and offerings)
- Other ministries
- The poor (alms)

Proverbs 19:17

17 He who has pity on the poor lends to the LORD, And He will pay back what he has given. (NKJ)

Proverbs 22:9

9 He who has a generous eye will be blessed, For he gives of his bread to the poor. (NKJ)

- Widows, fatherless (alms)

James 1:27

27 Pure and undefiled religion before God and the Father is this: to visit orphans and widows in their trouble, and to keep oneself unspotted from the world. (NKJ)

- Other Christians

Galatians 6:10

10 Therefore, as we have opportunity, let us do good to all, especially to those who are of the household of faith. (NKJ)

- As God moves on your heart, give to others.

Purpose - The Missing Link to Wealth

Notes

There is a supernatural connection between wealth and purpose. When the two are married, it opens the door for God's awesome power and anointing to bring great financial increase into your life.

In order to be wealthy in the Kingdom of God and be fully satisfied, believers must operate in their purpose. God foreordained and predestinated who we would be and our path in life. This path is where our anointing is. This is where our glory is. This is where the fullness of joy is. It means accomplishing the purpose of your life, which is being in the perfect will of God!

Ephesians 2:10

10 For we are God's (own) handiwork (His workmanship); recreated in Christ Jesus, (born anew) that we may do those good works which God predestined (planned beforehand) for us (taking paths which He prepared ahead of time), that we should walk in them (living the good life which He prearranged and made ready for us to live). (AMP)

Operating in the perfect will of God is operating in His presence all the time. The Psalmist said:

Psalm 16:11

11 "Thou wilt shew me the path of life: in thy presence is fulness of joy; at thy right hand there are pleasures for evermore." (KJV)

The reason Jesus said the path is narrow is that the way is fixed. Your purpose and destiny are pre-established; you are created with the ability to become wealthy through knowing your purpose and executing it to the fullest.

Notes

Purpose - The Missing Link to Wealth,
continued

Purpose is realized through the gift of work. Work glorifies God, which is why scripture says that to work is a gift from the Lord.

Ecclesiastes 5:19

19 Every man also to whom God hath given riches and wealth, and hath given him power to eat thereof, and to take his portion, and to rejoice in his labour; this is the gift of God. (KJV)

Business is the repository of wealth. When a believer asks, " where is the wealth stored up? " the primary answer is, "in business. " Major transfers will take place through business dealings. Every dollar, yen, euro, drachma, shekel, lira, franc, kugerand, deutch mark, and every other currency on earth is generated through the world of business.

The greatest seed you will ever sow is yourself. When you sow yourself into your God-given gift of work, you are certain to reap financial rewards and transfer wealth to yourself. The Word of God says that God will bless the work of your hands if you obey His commandments.

Deuteronomy 28:12

12 The LORD shall open unto thee his good treasure, the heaven to give the rain unto thy land in his season, and to bless all the work of thine hand: and thou shalt lend unto many nations, and thou shalt not borrow. (KJV)

Many times people do not succeed financially because they do not know their purpose. They chase fantasies or "get-rich-quick schemes. A "good deal" here and some "quick money" there have taken down many a Christian who succeeded at operating unbiblically and took a fall.

Tapping Into God's Economy

Proverbs 12:11

11 He who works his land will have abundant food, but he who chases fantasies lacks judgment.
(NIV)

Proverbs 28:19

19 He who works his land will have abundant food, but the one who chases fantasies will have his fill of poverty.
(NIV)

Conclusion Point

Many Christians do not know their purpose. Pray, seek God, and learn your purpose from the Holy Ghost and go to the wealthy place.

Notes

Workplace Wisdom Institute

Notes

Seedtime and Harvest

Seedtime and harvest shall not cease. When you plant seeds, you must wait a period of time then, God promises a harvest.

Genesis 8:22

22 While the earth remains, Seedtime and harvest, cold and heat, winter and summer, and day and night shall not cease. (NKJ)

2 Corinthians 9:10

10 Now may He who supplies seed to the sower, and bread for food, supply and multiply the seed you have sown and increase the fruits of your righteousness, (NKJ)

While most believers are familiar with the principle of seedtime and harvest, it is imperative that a discussion ensue. Beyond giving and receiving, seedtime and harvest is the next most potent spiritual financial principle.

Seedtime and harvest is a demonstration of how God operates supernaturally using natural forces which He has put in place. The process is progressive. The seed's potential is known fully in advance or in the beginning. Its maximum yield is also known, for we are told in scripture that a seed can reap up to 100-fold return. God has created every seed with supernatural power. Monetarily, every form of currency has the power to reproduce itself! Every seed has the power to yield after its own kind. This is found in Genesis 1:12.

Genesis 1:12

12 And the earth brought forth grass, the herb *that* yields seed accoding to its kind, and the tree that yields fruit, whose seed is in itself according to its kind. (NKJ)

Notes

If a seed has power, and God says He gives seed to the sower, then a believer can expect to get seed, take that powerful seed, sow it, and have manifold reproduction. What this all means is, that when seedtime is performed in obedience to God's Word and instruction, entering into the wealthy place can be a reality for every believer.

Supernaturally, God operates in the seed world. One definition for seedtime is "posterity." God sees the beginning from the end. He makes financial seed available for the believer to reap for posterity. God calls seedtime posterity because He sees financial resources available through 1000 generations!

Galatians 6:7

7 Do not be deceived, God is not mocked; for whatsoever a man sows, that he will also reap. (NKJ)

We understand this concept in the reverse because we know that if we steal God's money by not tithing or giving offerings, we enter into financial ruin. We also understand that when we do not put our hands to work, the Word of God goes so far as to say "we should not eat." Never mind the wealthy place.

2 Thessalonians 3:10

10 For even when we were with you, this we commanded you, that if any would not work, neither should he eat. (KJV)

Christians must "connect the dots" financially.

1 Corinthians 10:31

31 Whether therefore ye eat, or drink, or whatsoever ye do, do all to the glory of God. (NKJ)

Galatians 6:7

7 Be not deceived; God is not mocked: for whatsoever a man soweth, that shall he also reap. (NKJ)

Notes

Seedtime and Harvest, continued

The Spirit world is more powerful than the natural world.

Hebrews 11:3

3 Through faith we understand that the worlds were framed by the word of God, so that things which are seen were not made of things which do appear. (NKJ)

"You" put Laws into motion: natural actions trigger spiritual laws:

- Lack of diligence in spending = financial delays
- Lack of financial planning = hit & miss return
- Lack of financial research = financial disaster
- Slothfulness in business = no increase

First the natural then the spiritual.

1 Corinthians 15: 46

46 Howbeit that was not first which is spiritual, but that which is natural; and afterward that which is spiritual. (KJV)

Financial implications are tied to what you:

- Do, or
- Do not do

God is progressive with people.

A. God requires natural actions, which lead to supernatural interventions:

1. Preparing a budget and living by it
2. Faithfulness in payment of tithes and bills in a timely fashion
3. Investing knowledgeably, and allowing the Holy Spirit to guide you
4. Sowing sacrificially
5. Giving generously
6. Obeying God with all money and financial decisions

B. God requires steps of faith, which are demonstrated in natural acts, line upon line, precept upon precept. (Obedience to God when all information is not known is key and fundamental for God's intervention.)

C. God requires faithfulness in the little things BEFORE the big things.

Examples:

- The widow's pots of oil - 2 Kings 4:1-7
- Shunammite Woman - 2 Kings 4:8-37, 8:1-16
- Parable of the Talents - Luke 19:11-27
- Jesus said you must be faithful over the little things. - Matthew 25:21

Notes

Seedtime and Harvest, continued

Matthew 25:21

21 His lord said unto him, Well done, thou good and faithful servant: thou hast been faithful over a few things, I will make thee ruler over many things: enter thou into the joy of thy lord. (KJV)

Fundamental Truths About Finances

1. You must take natural steps if you expect the supernatural.

2. God moves progressively in everything He does.

3. Faithfulness and reward are incremental and integrally tied together.

4. After you have prayed and exercised your faith, (obedience, diligence, and contentment) natural work accelerates the intervention and reward of God.

5. You must know your purpose in this life.

6. The work of your hands can take you to the wealthy place.

YOU NEED A REVELATION OF WHEN TO HARVEST

Many people:

- Eat their seed.
- Eat the blade.
- Eat the ear and never get the harvest.

Mark 4:28-29

28 For the earth bringeth forth fruit of herself; first the blade, then the ear, after that the full corn in the ear.
29 But when the fruit is brought forth, immediately he putteth in the sickle, because the harvest is come. (KJV)

Paradigm Shift

Pray that God will reveal to you when and how to harvest.

Many believers reap their harvest prematurely. Some see the opportunity to increase but do not pray and seek God on whether it's God's ordained harvest time.

Prayer and direction from the Holy Spirit are paramount to knowing when the harvest is fully developed.

Whether it's a contract, a legal matter, a job offer, a business deal, selling stock, buying a house, selling a house, or a real estate investment, you MUST hear from God on timing.

Romans 8:14

14 For as many as are led by the Spirit of God, these are sons of God. (NKJ)

Notes

Notes

Seedtime and Harvest, continued

Sources of Harvest:

- Inheritance and Gifts - usually not enough
- Business - unlimited resource
- Government Entitlements and Assistance - temporary
- Borrow - bondage
- Steal - sin

All money is transferred through business. Business is where the wealth is.

You are a business!

A few ways money gets transferred:

- Sow into the church
- Gifts
- Inheritance
- Find money in the street
- Steal
- Business

1. **Sowing into the Church**

   Sowing tithes and offerings sets the spiritual stage. You must act in the natural to invoke the supernatural.

2. **Gifts**

   The amount never seems to be enough.

3. **Inheritance**

   Most inheritances are consumed in three months. Superannuation (donors outliving their money).

4. **Finding Money on the Street**

   Limited and unpredictable

5. **Stealing**

   An abomination to God

   Limited option – leads to jail, loss of life, physical harm, etc.

6. **Business**

   Unlimited Potential
   $1.00
   $10.00
   $100.00
   $1,000.00
   $10,000.00
   $100,000.00
   $1,000,000.00

Notes

Financial Stewardship Principle in Business

Matthew 25:21

21 His lord said to him, Well *done,* good and faithful servant; you were faithful over a few things, I will make you ruler over many things. Enter into the joy of your lord. (NKJ)

Luke 19:13

13 So he called ten of his servants, delivered to them ten minas, and said to them, 'Do business till I come.' (NKJ)

Notes

Seedtime – Harvesting Money, continued

Paradigm Shift
Business is the source of all financial transfers. In order for substantial dollars to be transferred to believers, they must be involved in business.

Tithes and Offerings

Notes

Principle

God requires you to give tithes and offerings.

Definition of the Tithe:

The first 10% of income (Malachi 3:10)

Definition of an Offering:

A gift or contribution above your tithe given to your local church or another ministry.

Malachi 3:8-12

8 Will a man rob God? Yet you have robbed Me!
But you say, 'In what way have we robbed You?'
In tithes and offerings.
9 You are cursed with a curse, for you have
robbed Me, even this whole nation.
10 Bring all the tithes into the storehouse, that
there may be food in My house, and try Me now
in this," says the Lord of hosts, "If I will not open for
you the windows of heaven and pour out for you
such blessing that there will not be room enough
to receive it.
11 "And I will rebuke the devourer for your sakes,
so that he will not destroy the fruit of your ground,
nor shall the vine fail to bear fruit for you in the
field," says the Lord of hosts;
12 "And all nations will call you blessed, for you
will be a delightful land," says the Lord of hosts.
(NKJ)

Leviticus 27:30

30 And all the tithe of the land, whether of the seed of the land or of the fruit of the tree, is the Lord's. It is holy to the Lord. (NKJ)

Notes

Tithes and Offerings, continued

Matthew 23:23

23 "Woe to you, scribes and Pharisees, hypocrites! For you pay tithe of mint and anise and cummin, and have neglected the weightier matters of the law: justice and mercy and faith. These you ought to have done, without leaving the others undone. (NKJ)

All money belongs to God.

- The tithe is Holy unto God.
- The tithe goes to your local church.
- You should be giving offerings to your local church.
- Offerings should go to other ministries also.

Scriptural Implications

- God will bless you tremendously when you tithe.
- If you don't tithe, you are robbing God. (Malachi 3:10)
- God will honor you when you give tithes and offerings.
- God will protect your finances. (Malachi 3:11)
- Tithing obligates God to be involved in your financial welfare.

Practical Implications

- You will have increase.
- If God cannot trust you to properly manage 10% of His holy money, He cannot trust you to manage larger sums.
- God will meet your needs even in the face of adversity.

Notes

Practical Application
Tithe to your local church.

Tithe as a percentage of the gross - not the net of all income.

Example:

Monthly Gross Income:	**$1,000.00**
Taxes	-$200.00
Insurance	-$50.00
Net Income:	$750.00
Tithe:	**$100.00**

Note: When you tithe from the gross, you do not need to tithe from your income tax check.

Do it joyfully

2 Corinthians 9:7

7 So let each one give as he purposes in his heart, not grudgingly or of necessity; for God loves a cheerful giver. (NKJ)

Workplace Wisdom Institute

Notes

Tithes and Offerings, continued

Pay tithes first before paying bills and debts.

- Do not neglect the tithe for bills.
- Set aside your tithe money immediately.

Give offerings as God directs you.

Scriptural Implications

- God gives seed to the sower.
- You have to allow time to pass for the benefits to be manifested.
- God promises a harvest.

Practical Implications

- You must plant a seed to get a harvest.
- Don't always expect immediate results.
- You should expect a harvest.
- Giving to Christian causes builds up the body of Christ.

Practical Application

Be patient.

Be generous.

Focus on giving to Christian causes.

Module

Study Questions

1. "Give and it will be given to you good measure, pressed down, shaken together,"... is found in:
   A) 2 Corinthians 9:6
   B) Proverbs 11:25
   C) Luke 6:38
   D) James 1:27

2. All of the following are principles of financial increase except:
   A) Integrity
   B) Not trusting God
   C) Honoring the Lord with possessions
   D) Diligence

3. Giving is more important than receiving.
   A) True
   B) False

4. "He who is slothful in his work is a brother to him who is a great destroyer," is found in:
   A) Proverbs 11:25
   B) Proverbs 3:9
   C) Proverbs 10:4
   D) Proverbs 18:9

5. "While the earth remains, seed time and harvest, cold and heat, winter and summer," .... is found in:
   A) 2 Corinthians 9:6
   B) Proverbs 11:25
   C) Luke 6:38
   D) Genesis 8:22

6. The scripture that states that the tithe is holy to the Lord is found in:
   A) Malachi 3:8-12
   B) 2 Corinthians 9:10
   C) Proverbs 11:25
   D) Leviticus 27:30

Module

Study Questions, continued

7. All of the following about tithing is true except:
   A) God will bless you tremendously when you tithe.
   B) God will protect your finances when you tithe.
   C) Your tithe can go to any ministry that feeds you the Word of God.
   D) God will honor you when you tithe.

8. When understanding and applying the principle of seedtime and harvest you should consider all of the following except:
   A) God promises a harvest.
   B) You must plant a seed to get a harvest.
   C) Most harvests are immediately manifested.
   D) God gives seed to the sower.
   E) Giving to Christian causes builds up the Body of Christ.

9. All of the following are causes of financial ruin except:
   A) Wickedness
   B) Loving pleasure
   C) Ignoring correction
   D) Hard work

10. "The hand of the diligent will rule," is found in:
    A) Proverbs 12:24
    B) Proverbs 21:5
    C) Proverbs 10:4
    D) Proverbs 28:19

11. All of the following about tithing is true except:
    A) The tithe goes to your local church.
    B) Tithe off of your net income.
    C) You should tithe joyfully.
    D) Pay tithes first before paying bills or debts.

Tapping Into God's Economy

12. You should give to:
    A) The poor
    B) Your local church
    C) Widows and the fatherless
    D) Other ministries
    E) All of the above

13. ___________ is the primary reason most people are in financial trouble.
    A) Discontentment
    B) Diligence
    C) Contentment
    D) Generosity

14. "Now godliness with contentment is great gain," is found in:
    A) Philippians 4:11
    B) Hebrews 13:5
    C) 1 Timothy 6:6
    D) Proverbs 21:25

15. "He who tills his land will be satisfied with bread, but he who follows frivolity is devoid of understanding," is found in:
    A) Proverbs 12:24
    B) Proverbs 21:5
    C) Proverbs 10:4
    D) Proverbs 12:11

16. "Pride goes before destruction and a haughty spirit before a fall," is found in:
    A) Proverbs 16:18
    B) Proverbs 21:17
    C) Proverbs 23:21
    D) Proverbs 18:18

17. Lack of contentment causes a person to buy more than they need and results in destructive behavior.
    A) True
    B) False

Module

Study Questions, continued

18. All of the following are causes of financial ruin except:
    A) Talking too much
    B) Pride
    C) Trusting God
    D) Chasing fantasies

19. A tithe is a gift or contribution above your offering given to your local church or another ministry.
    A) True
    B) False

20. "But I say: he who sows sparingly will also reap sparingly, and he who sows bountifully will also reap bountifully," is found in:
    A) 2 Corinthians 9:6
    B) Proverbs 11:25
    C) Luke 6:38
    D) James 1:27

Principles of Financial Ruin and Increase

Principles of Financial Ruin and Increase

Many times believers find themselves "doing all the right things" when it comes to spiritual requirements as set forth in the Bible. For example, they sow seed, name the seed, pay their tithes, and give offerings; yet, they are not experiencing multiplied financial growth.

This chapter is devoted to revealing behaviors that will impact your financial growth. The Bible has a lot to say about behavior that affects you financially. Christians make conscious decisions daily, all day long, that either positively or negatively affect their financial health. Many times these decisions are made with no awareness of the financial ramifications.

Behaviors that lead to financial ruin include:

- Wickedness
- Pride
- Ignoring Correction
- Laziness
- Talking Too Much
- Impatience
- Chasing Fantasies

Conversely, you can experience increase in your finances if you put into practice the principles that lead to financial gain, such as:

- Honoring the Lord with possessions
- Integrity
- Diligence and Hard Work
- Contentment
- Generosity

Principles of Financial Ruin and Increase

This chapter delves into the day-to-day aspects of the Christian walk. One can begin to see when manifestation is evident or if correction must be taken. However, the student who hearkens to the Word of God shall surely prosper. Developing character is essential to financial growth for the Kingdom of God.

I think it would be a good idea if business colleges would include the Bible in their list of textbooks. I suppose its value lies in the fact that it teaches character. J.C. Penney

Notes

Principles of Financial Ruin

A. Wickedness

Proverbs 11:5

5 The righteousness of the blameless will direct his way aright, but the wicked will fall by his own wickedness. (NKJ)

Proverbs 14:11

11 The house of the wicked will be overthrown, but the tent of the upright will flourish. (NKJ)

Proverbs 21:12

12 The righteous God wisely considers the house of the wicked, overthrowing the wicked for their wickedness. (NKJ)

Wisdom Point
Breaches of integrity will lead to financial ruin. They will impact your ability to prosper financially from God's perspective.

Why does God hate wickedness? One reason is because it opens the door to satanic involvement. Satan has the ability to influence the resources that the individual is managing or stewarding.

Examples of wickedness

1. Lying

Proverbs12:22

22 **Lying** lips are an abomination to the LORD, but those who deal truthfully are His delight.(NKJ)

Proverbs12:22

22 **Lying** lips are extremely disgusting and hateful to the Lord, but they who deal faithfully are His delight. (AMP)

Proverbs 6:16-19

16 These six things the LORD hates, yes, seven are an abomination to Him:
17 A proud look, a **lying** tongue, hands that shed innocent blood,
18 A heart that devises wicked plans, feet that are swift in running to evil,
19 A false witness who speaks **lies**, and one who sows discord among brethren. (NKJ)

Revelation 21:8

8 But the cowardly, unbelieving, abominable, murderers, sexually immoral, sorcerers, idolaters, and all **liars** shall have their part in the lake which burns with fire and brimstone, which is the second death." (NKJ)

2. Cheating and Stealing

Stealing is to take or transfer the stewardship of another's property without their permission or consent either secretly or by force.

Exodus 20:15

15 You shall not **steal**. (NKJ)

Leviticus 6:2-4

2 If a person sins and commits a trespass against the LORD by lying to his neighbor about what was delivered to him for safekeeping, or about a pledge, or about a robbery, or if he has extorted from his neighbor,
3 or if he has found what was lost and lies concerning it, and swears falsely—in any one of these things that a man may do in which he sins:
4 then it shall be, because he has sinned and is guilty, that he shall restore what he has **stolen**, or the thing which he has extorted, or what was delivered to him for safekeeping, or the lost thing which he found, (NKJ)

Notes

Principles of Financial Ruin, continued

1 Corinthians 6:7-11

7 Now therefore, it is already an utter failure for
you that you go to law against one another. Why
do you not rather accept wrong? Why do you
not rather let yourselves be cheated?
8 No, you yourselves do wrong and **cheat**, and
you do these things to your brethren!
9 Do you not know that the unrighteous will not
inherit the kingdom of God? Do not be deceived. Neither fornicators, nor idolaters, nor
adulterers, nor homosexuals, nor sodomites,
10 nor **thieves**, nor covetous, nor drunkards, nor
revilers, nor extortioners will inherit the kingdom of
God.
11 And such were some of you. But you were
washed, but you were sanctified, but you were
justified in the name of the Lord Jesus and by the
Spirit of our God. (NKJ)

3. Fornication (sexual immorality)

1 Corinthians 6:13

13 Foods for the stomach and the stomach for foods, but God will destroy both it and them. Now the **body is not for sexual immorality** but for the Lord, and the Lord for the body. (NKJ)

1 Corinthians 6:18

18 **Flee sexual immorality**. Every sin that a man does is outside the body, but he who commits sexual immorality sins against his own body. (NKJ)

Galatians 5:19

19 Now the works of the flesh are evident, which are: adultery, **fornication**, uncleanness, lewdness, … (NKJ)

Notes

Ephesians 5:3-5

3 But **fornication** and all uncleanness or covetousness, let it not even be named among you, as
is fitting for saints;
4 neither filthiness, nor foolish talking, nor coarse
jesting, which are not fitting, but rather giving of
thanks.
5 For this you know, that no **fornicator**, unclean
person, nor covetous man, who is an idolater, has
any inheritance in the kingdom of Christ and
God. (NKJ)

Revelations 21:7-8

7 He who overcomes shall inherit all things, and I
will be his God and he shall be My son.
8 But the cowardly, unbelieving, abominable,
murderers, **sexually immoral**, sorcerers, idolaters,
and all liars shall have their part in the lake which
burns with fire and brimstone, which is the second
death." (NKJ)

Revelations 21:14-15

14 Blessed are those who do His commandments, that they may have the right to the tree of
life, and may enter through the gates into the
city.
15 But outside are dogs and sorcerers and **sexually immoral** and murderers and idolaters, and
whoever loves and practices a lie." (NKJ)

Colossians 3:5

5 Therefore put to death your members which
are on the earth: **fornication**, uncleanness, passion, evil desire, and covetousness, which is
idolatry. (NKJ)

1 Thessalonians 4:3-5

3 For this is the will of God, your sanctification:
that you should abstain from **sexual immorality**;
4 that each of you should know how to possess
his own vessel in sanctification and honor,
5 not in passion of lust, like the Gentiles who do
not know God; (NKJ)

Notes

Principles of Financial Ruin, continued

4. Adultery

Exodus 20:14

14 You shall not commit **adultery**. (NKJ)

Proverbs 5:3-10

3 For the lips of an **immoral woman** drip honey, and her mouth is smoother than oil;
4 But in the end she is bitter as wormwood, sharp as a two-edged sword.
5 Her feet go down to death, her steps lay hold of hell.
6 Lest you ponder her path of life—her ways are unstable; you do not know them.
7 Therefore hear me now, my children, and do not depart from the words of my mouth.
8 Remove your way far from her, and do not go near the door of her house,
9 Lest you give your honor to others, and your years to the cruel one;
10 Lest aliens be filled with your wealth, and your labors go to the house of a foreigner; (NKJ)

Proverbs 6:32

32 Whoever commits **adultery** with a woman lacks understanding; he who does so destroys his own soul. (NKJ)

Matthew 5:27-28

27 You have heard that it was said to those of old, 'You shall not commit **adultery**.'
28 But I say to you that whoever looks at a woman to lust for her has already committed **adultery** with her in his heart. (NKJ)

5. Substance abuse

Notes

Proverbs 20:1

1 Wine is a mocker, **strong drink** is a brawler, and whoever is led astray by it is not wise. (NKJ)

Proverbs 21:17

17 He who loves pleasure will be a poor man; he who **loves wine** and oil will not be rich. (NKJ)

Proverbs 23:29-35

29 Who has woe? Who has sorrow? Who has contentions? Who has complaints? Who has wounds without cause? Who has redness of eyes?
30 Those who **linger long at the wine**, those who go in search of mixed wine.
31 Do not look on the wine when it is red, when it sparkles in the cup, when it swirls around smoothly;
32 At the last it bites like a serpent, and stings like a viper.
33 Your eyes will see strange things, and your heart will utter perverse things.
34 Yes, you will be like one who lies down in the midst of the sea, or like one who lies at the top of the mast, saying:
35 "They have struck me, but I was not hurt; they have beaten me, but I did not feel it. When shall I awake, that I may seek another drink?" (NKJ)

Proverbs 23:20-21

20 Do not mix with winebibbers, or with gluttonous eaters of meat;
21 For the **drunkard** and the glutton will come to poverty, and drowsiness will clothe a man with rags. (NKJ)

Ephesians 5:18

18 **Do not get drunk on wine**, which leads to debauchery. Instead, be filled with the Spirit. (NIV)

Notes

Principles of Financial Ruin, continued

6. God will deal with wicked people.

Psalm 73:2-19

2 But as for me, my feet had almost slipped; I had
nearly lost my foothold.
3 For I envied the arrogant when I saw the prosperity of the wicked.
4 They have no struggles; their bodies are
healthy and strong.
5 They are free from the burdens common to
man; they are not plagued by human ills.
6 Therefore pride is their necklace; they clothe
themselves with violence.
7 From their callous hearts comes iniquity; the evil
conceits of their minds know no limits.
8 They scoff, and speak with malice; in their
arrogance they threaten oppression.
9 Their mouths lay claim to heaven, and their
tongues take possession of the earth.
10 Therefore their people turn to them and drink
up waters in abundance.
11 They say, "How can God know? Does the
Most High have knowledge?"
12 This is what the wicked are like— always care-
free, they increase in wealth.
13 Surely in vain have I kept my heart pure; in
vain have I washed my hands in innocence.
14 All day long I have been plagued; I have
been punished every morning.
15 If I had said, "I will speak thus," I would have
betrayed your children.
16 When I tried to understand all this, it was op-
pressive to me
17 till I entered the sanctuary of God; then I
understood their final destiny.
18 Surely you place them on slippery ground; you
cast them down to ruin.
19 How suddenly are they destroyed, completely
swept away by terrors! (NIV)

Conclusion Point
Wickedness will prevent the anointing of God from being manifested in your life.

Notes

B. Talking too much

Proverbs 10:8

8 The wise in heart accept commands, but **a chattering fool** comes to ruin. (NIV)

Proverbs 14:23

23 In all labor there is profit, but **idle chatter** leads only to poverty. (NKJ)

Proverbs 18:6-8

6 A **fool's lips** bring him strife, and his mouth invites a beating.
7 A fool's mouth is his undoing, and his lips are a snare to his soul.
8 The **words of a gossip** are like choice morsels; they go down to a man's inmost parts. (NIV)

Proverbs 17:27-28

27 He who has knowledge spares his words, and a man of understanding is of a calm spirit.
28 Even a fool is counted wise when he holds his peace; when he shuts his lips, he is considered perceptive. (NKJ)

Proverbs 20:19

19 A **gossip** betrays a confidence; so avoid a man who talks too much. (NIV)

Ephesians 5:4

4 neither filthiness, nor **foolish talking**, nor coarse jesting, which are not fitting, but rather giving of thanks. (NKJ)

Ephesians 4:29

29 Do not let any **unwholesome talk** come out of your mouths, but only what is helpful for building others up according to their needs, that it may benefit those who listen. (NIV)

Notes

Principles of Financial Ruin, continued

Colossians 3:8-10

8 But now you yourselves are to put off all these:
anger, wrath, malice, blasphemy, **filthy language**
out of your mouth.
9 Do not lie to one another, since you have put
off the old man with his deeds,
10 and have put on the new man who is renewed in knowledge according to the image of
Him who created him, (NKJ)

C. Ignoring Correction

Three types of instruction:

1. Instruction in righteousness

2. Instruction in personal growth and development
   a. attitude
   b. character (behavior)
   c. human interactions and relationships

3. Instruction in job skills

Proverbs 12:1

1 Whoever loves instruction loves knowledge, but
he who hates correction is stupid.
(NKJ)

Proverbs 9:8-9

8 **Do not correct a scoffer**, lest he hate you;
rebuke a wise man, and he will love you.
9 Give instruction to a wise man, and he will be
still wiser; teach a just man, and he will increase in
learning. (NKJ)

Proverbs 10:17

17 He who keeps instruction is in the way of life,
but **he who refuses correction goes astray**. (NKJ)

Proverbs13:18

18 Poverty and shame will come to him who disdains **correction**, but he who regards a rebuke will be honored. (NKJ)

Proverbs 15:10

10 Harsh discipline is for him who forsakes the way, and **he who hates correction will die**. (NKJ)

Proverbs 15:31-32

31 He who listens to a life-giving rebuke will be at home among the wise.
32 He who ignores discipline despises himself, but whoever heeds **correction** gains understanding. (NIV)

D. Pride

Psalm 138:6

6 Though the LORD is on high, yet He regards the lowly; but the proud He knows from afar. (NKJ)

Proverbs 13:10

10 Pride only breeds quarrels, but wisdom is found in those who take advice. (NIV)

Proverbs 16:5

5 Everyone **proud in heart** is an abomination to the LORD; though they join forces, none will go unpunished. (NKJ)

Proverbs 16:18

18 **Pride goes before destruction**, and a haughty spirit before a fall. (NKJ)

Jeremiah 9:23-24

23 This is what the LORD says: "Let not the wise man boast of his wisdom or the strong man boast of his strength or the rich man boast of his riches,
24 but let him who boasts boast about this: that he understands and knows me, that I am the LORD, who exercises kindness, justice and righteousness on earth, for in these I delight," declares the LORD. (NIV)

Notes

Principles of Financial Ruin, continued

E. Impatience

Proverbs 21:5

5 The plans of the diligent lead surely to plenty, but those of everyone who is **hasty**, surely to poverty. (NKJ)

Proverbs 19:2

2 It is not good to have zeal without knowledge, nor to be **hasty** and miss the way. (NIV)

Proverbs 20:21

21 An inheritance **gained hastily** at the beginning will not be blessed at the end. (NKJ)

Proverbs 28:22

22 A man with an evil eye hastens after riches, and does not consider that poverty will come upon him. (NKJ)

Proverbs 28:20

20 A faithful man will abound with blessings, but he who hastens to be rich will not go unpunished. (NKJ)

1 Timothy 6:9

9 But those who desire to be rich fall into temptation and a snare, and into many foolish and harmful lusts which drown men in destruction and perdition. (NKJ)

F. Laziness

Notes

Proverbs 24:30-34

30 I went by the field of the **lazy** man, and by the
vineyard of the man devoid of understanding;
31 And there it was, all overgrown with thorns; its
surface was covered with nettles; its stone wall
was broken down.
32 When I saw it, I considered it well; I looked on it
and received instruction:
33 A little sleep, a little slumber, a little folding of
the hands to rest;
34 So shall your poverty come like a prowler, and
your need like an armed man. (NKJ)

Proverbs 12:24

24 The hand of the diligent will rule, but the **lazy** man will be put to forced labor.
(NKJ)

Proverbs 18:9

9 One who is slack in his work is brother to one who destroys. (NIV)

Proverbs 20:13

13 Do not love sleep or you will grow poor; stay awake and you will have food to spare. (NIV)

G. Chasing Fantasies

Proverbs 12:11

11 He who works his land will have abundant food, but he who **chases fantasies** lacks judgment. (NIV)

Proverbs 28:19

19 He who works his land will have abundant food, but the one who **chases fantasies** will have his fill of poverty. (NIV)

Notes

Principles of Increase

A. Honoring the Lord with possessions

Proverbs 3:9-10

9 Honor the LORD with your possessions, and with the firstfruits of all your increase;
10 So your barns will be filled with plenty, and your vats will overflow with new wine. (NKJ)

B. Trusting God

Proverbs 22:4

4 By humility and the fear of the LORD are riches and honor and life. (NKJ)

Proverbs 10:22

22 The blessing of the LORD makes one rich, and He adds no sorrow with it. (NKJ)

Proverbs 28:25

25 He who is of a proud heart stirs up strife, but he who **trusts in the LORD** will be prospered. (NKJ)

C. Generosity

Proverbs 11:25

25 A generous man will prosper; he who refreshes others will himself be refreshed. (NIV)

D. Integrity

Notes

Psalm 37:23-29

23 The steps of a good man are ordered by the
LORD, and He delights in his way.
24 Though he fall, he shall not be utterly cast
down; for the LORD upholds him with His hand.
25 I have been young, and now am old; yet I
have not seen the righteous forsaken, nor his
descendants begging bread.
26 He is ever merciful, and lends; and his descendants are blessed.
27 Depart from evil, and do good; and dwell
forevermore.
28 For the LORD loves justice, and does not
forsake His saints; they are preserved forever, but
the descendants of the wicked shall be cut off.
29 The righteous shall inherit the land, and dwell
in it forever. (NKJ)

Psalm 15:1-5

1 LORD, who may abide in Your tabernacle?
Who may dwell in Your holy hill?
2 He who walks uprightly, and works righteousness, and speaks the truth in his heart;
3 He who does not backbite with his tongue, nor
does evil to his neighbor, nor does he take up a
reproach against his friend;
4 In whose eyes a vile person is despised, but he
honors those who fear the LORD; he who swears
to his own hurt and does not change;
5 He who does not put out his money at usury,
nor does he take a bribe against the innocent.
He who does these things shall never be moved.
(NKJ)

Proverbs 10:9

9 The man of **integrity** walks securely, but he who takes crooked paths will be found out. (NIV)

Proverbs 11:3

3 The integrity of the upright guides them, but the unfaithful are destroyed by their duplicity. (NIV)

Notes

Principles of Increase, continued

Proverbs 11:5

5 The righteousness of the blameless makes a
straight way for them, but the wicked are
brought down by their own wickedness. (NIV)

Proverbs 21:3

3 To do what is right and just is more acceptable
to the LORD than sacrifice. (NIV)

Isaiah 33:15-16

15 He who walks righteously and speaks what is
right, who rejects gain from extortion and keeps
his hand from accepting bribes, who stops his
ears against plots of murder and shuts his eyes
against contemplating evil—
16 this is the man who will dwell on the heights,
whose refuge will be the mountain fortress. His
bread will be supplied, and water will not fail him.
(NIV)

Ecclesiastes 2:26

26 To the man who pleases him, God gives wisdom, knowledge and happiness, but to the sinner he gives the task of gathering and storing up wealth to hand it over to the one who pleases God. This too is meaningless, a chasing after the wind. (NIV)

Principles of Financial Ruin and Increase

Diligence and Hard Work

Definition of diligence:

Steady in application to business; constant in effort or exertion to accomplish what is undertaken; attentive; industrious; not idle; or negligent exertion.

(Random House Dictionary of the English Language, Random House, 2nd Ed., New York, 1984, page 554.)

Proverbs 10:4

4 He who has a slack hand becomes poor, but the hand of the diligent makes rich. (NKJ)

Proverbs 12:24

24 The hand of the diligent will rule, but the lazy man will be put to forced labor. (NKJ)

Proverbs 13:4

4 The soul of the lazy man desires, and has nothing; but the soul of the diligent shall be made rich. (NKJ)

Proverbs 13:11

11 Wealth *gained* by dishonesty wil be diminished, But he who gathers by labor will increase. (NKJ)

Proverbs 14:23

23 In all labor there is profit, but idle chatter leads only to poverty. (NKJ)

Proverbs 21:5

5 The plans of the diligent lead surely to plenty, but those of everyone who is hasty, surely to poverty. (NKJ)

Practical Implications

- Hard work produces financial gain.
- Opportunity will present itself when you are diligent (work hard).

Notes

Principles of Increase, continued

Practical Application

Go to work, be on time, and work hard.

Give an honest days work.

Proverbs 21:25-26

25 The desire of the lazy man kills him, for his
hands refuse to labor.
26 He covets greedily all day long, but the righteous gives and does not spare. (NKJ)

Contentment

Definition of contentment:

To be satisfied; to satisfy the mind of; to make quiet, so as to stop complaint or opposition (Random House Dictionary of the English Language, Random House, 2nd Ed., New York, 1984, page 439.)

Hebrews 13:5

5 Let your conduct be without covetousness; be content with such things as you have. For He Himself has said, "I will never leave you nor forsake you." (NKJ)

Philippians 4:11-13

11 Not that I speak in regard to need, for I have learned in whatever state I am, to be content:
12 I know how to be abased, and I know how to abound. Everywhere and in all things I have learned both to be full and to be hungry, both to abound and to suffer need.
13 I can do all things through Christ who strengthens me. (NKJ)

1 Timothy 6:6-10

6 Now godliness with contentment is great gain.
7 For we brought nothing into this world, and it is certain we can carry nothing out.
8 And having food and clothing, with these we shall be content.
9 But those who desire to be rich fall into temptation and a snare, and into many foolish and harmful lusts which drown men in destruction and perdition.
10 For the love of money is a root of all kinds of evil, for which some have strayed from the faith in their greediness, and pierced themselves through with many sorrows. (NKJ)

Notes

Notes

Principles of Increase, continued

Practical Implications

- Lack of contentment causes you to buy more than you need and causes destructive behavior.
- Contentment brings joy and a sense of fulfillment.
- Discontentment is the primary reason most people are in financial trouble and have poor self-esteem issues.

Practical Application
Stop comparing yourself to others.

Stop trying to keep up with the "Joneses".

2 Corinthians 10:12

12 For we dare not class ourselves or compare ourselves with those who commend themselves. But they, measuring themselves by themselves, and comparing themselves among themselves, are not wise. (NKJ)

Practical Application
Understand that advertising stimulates discontent.

Notes

Avoid all "get-rich-quick" schemes (greed), such as:

a. Lottery

b. Gambling

c. Pyramid schemes

d. Other schemes (if it sounds too good to be true, it is.)

We must build on the correct foundation.

Matthew 7:24-27

24 Therefore whoever hears these sayings of
Mine, and does them, I will liken him to a wise
man who built his house on the rock:
25 and the rain descended, the floods came,
and the winds blew and beat on that house; and
it did not fall, for it was founded on the rock.
26 Now everyone who hears these sayings of
Mine, and does not do them, will be like a foolish
man who built his house on the sand:
27 and the rain descended, the floods came,
and the winds blew and beat on that house; and
it fell. And great was its fall. (NKJ)

Psalm 112:1-3

1 Praise the LORD! Blessed is the man who fears
the LORD, who delights greatly in His commandments.
2 His descendants will be mighty on earth; the
generation of the upright will be blessed.
3 Wealth and riches will be in his house, and his
righteousness endures forever. (NKJ)

Notes

Budgeting

for

Kingdom Living

Workplace Wisdom Institute

Budgeting for Kingdom Living

In the Gospel according to Luke 14:28–30, Jesus admonishes us to determine our financial exposure prior to undertaking projects: "For which of you, intending to build a tower, sitteth not down first, and counteth the cost, whether he have sufficient to finish it? Lest haply, after he hath laid the foundation, and is not able to finish it, all that behold it begin to mock him saying, "This man began to build, and was not able to finish." (KJV)

In order to count the cost, one must design a financial plan for future events. Whether it is taking care of oneself, getting married, buying a home, having children, traveling, having more than enough seed to sow, caring for elderly parents, college education, studying abroad, slowing down later in life or starting a business. For all of these desires, planning is required. If one does not plan, the likelihood of successfully accomplishing objectives is remote or hit or miss, at best.

The Word of God tells us to have a vision so that we do not perish (Proverbs 29:18). It instructs us to write the vision and make it plain so that he who reads it may run (Habakkuk 2:2). ***Money Dominators*** are running with a plan!

Many in the Body of Christ are floundering financially because they don't have a written, documented plan of action for their finances. The first and fundamental step towards domination is to develop a budget. A budget is a plan, which identifies financial goals and objectives. It examines revenue sources and expenditure outflows to determine the viability and feasibility of goals in a realistic timetable.

At work, on project management teams, this process is highly accepted. Yet, when it comes to our personal finances, most people fall far short of God's plan for their money. Planning time is never lost time.

What would the world look like if every parent sat down with their children and laid out a planning process for the family finances? How many financial blunders could be avoided or averted if financial planning was an integral part of every believer's life. **Believers ought to Dominate Money on purpose, not by accident!**

Workplace Wisdom Institute

Budgeting for Kingdom Living

There is no shortage of money. The world tragedy of September 11, 2001 proved that. In a few short weeks, over a billion dollars was raised, seemingly "over night." The people who gave did not go bankrupt due to their giving. They had enough money stashed away to give and help countless others.

Many in the Body of Christ say they do not have any money. Yet, if we were to examine how much money has gone through their hands, they would be amazed. For example, if a person made just $20,000 per year (with no raise or adjustments for inflation) over 20 years, s/he would have managed $400,000. A couple who made a combined salary of $75,000 per year (with no raise or inflation adjustments), would have managed $1,500,000 over 20 years.

The average individual's work life spans 40 years (from 25 years of age to 65). At this rate, the person who made just $20,000 (with no adjustments), would have managed $800,000 more than three-quarters of a million dollars. The couple making $75,000 (with no raise and no adjustments for inflation), would have managed $3,000,000.

Both scenarios, conservatively adjusted for 20% of their earnings, saved, over the course of a 40-year period, at the rate of 7% would yield the following:

Yearly Salary	40 Years Earnings Earnings (no adjs.)	20% of Gross Wages Saved Per Year	20% Saved Over 40 Years @ 7% Cum.
$20,000	$ 800,000	$ 4,000	$ 858,438
$75,000	$3,000,000	$15,000	$3,219,145

It is important for believers to understand that significant sums of money go through their hands, and that managing and saving money through a comprehensive financial plan, including budgeting, could yield substantial gain over time, when impacted by the Law of Compounding Interest.

Preparation time pays great dividends!

Workplace Wisdom Institute

Notes

How to Maximize Money

Plan and Prepare

Planning and preparation time is never lost time.

Proverbs 16:3

3 Roll your works upon the Lord (commit and trust them wholly to Him; He will cause your thoughts to become agreeable to His will, and) so shall your plans be established and succeed. (AMP)

Luke 14:28-30

28 For which of you, intending to build a tower, does not sit down first and count the cost, whether he has enough to finish it—
29 lest, after he has laid the foundation, and is not able to finish, all who see it begin to mock him,
30 saying, 'This man began to build and was not able to finish.' (NKJ)

Habakkuk 2:2

2 Then the Lord answered me and said: "Write the vision and make it plain on tablets, that he may run who reads it. (NKJ)

1 Corinthians 14:40

40 Let all things be done decently and in order. (NKJ)

Budgeting for Kingdom Living

Live below your income.

Notes

Wisdom Point

The key to financial increase is to live below your income.

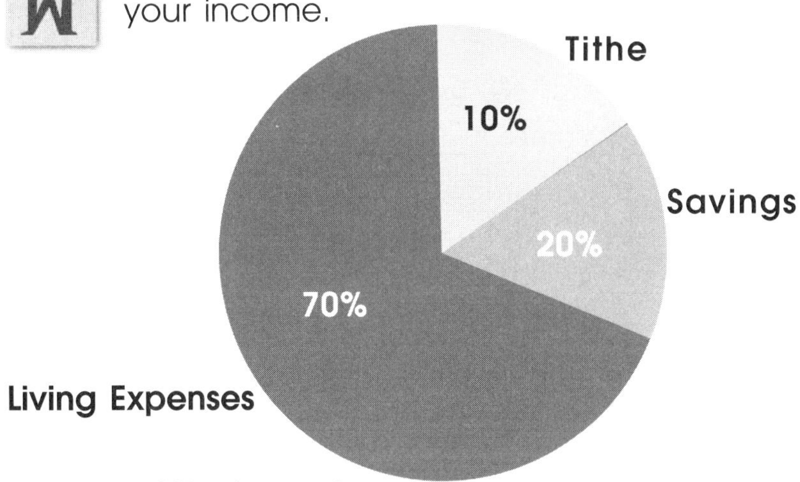

Live on 70% of your income.

The average family spends significantly more than it earns each year.

Set aside 10% for the tithe.

Malachi 3:10

10 Bring all the tithes into the storehouse, that there may be food in My house, and try Me now in this," says the Lord of hosts, "If I will not open for you the windows of heaven and pour out for you such blessing that there will not be room enough to receive it. (NKJ)

Set aside 20% for savings.

You should save.

Proverbs 6:6-8

6 Go to the ant, you sluggard; consider its ways and be wise!
7 It has no commander, no overseer or ruler,
8 yet it stores its provisions in summer and gathers its food at harvest. (NIV)

Notes

How to Maximize Money, continued

Joseph advised Pharaoh to save 20%.

Genesis 41:34-36

34 Let Pharaoh do this, and let him appoint
officers over the land, to collect one-fifth (20%)
of the produce of the land of Egypt in the seven
plentiful years.
35 And let them gather all the food of those
good years that are coming, and store up grain
under the authority of Pharaoh, and let them
keep food in the cities.
36 Then that food shall be as a reserve for the
land for the seven years of famine which shall be
in the land of Egypt, that the land may not perish
during the famine. (NKJ)

Short-term savings:

- The goal is to have six months of living expenses saved.
- This is considered an emergency fund and should not be tapped unless absolutely necessary. It should remain relatively liquid. (See Investment Section)

Long Term Savings:

- We must save to provide a godly inheritance for our children and grandchildren.

Proverbs 19:14a

14 Houses and riches are an inheritance from fathers, (NKJ)

Proverbs 13:22a

22 A good man leaves an inheritance to his children's children, (NKJ)

Note: This is a goal. It may take time to achieve. Start setting aside something now.

Notes

Notes

Budgeting

Definition of Budget:
A plan for spending money

The Purpose of a Budget is to:

- Control spending.
- Provide an opportunity to pray about income and spending decisions.
- Use as a money-management tool to make wise spending decisions and/or expense reductions.

The budget must be tailor-made to fit your finances, and it can be handwritten or computerized.

How to Budget

- Review prior years' income and expenses.
- Determine how money is currently being spent (by category).
- Compute your net wages and/or income.
- Analyze the information in a spreadsheet.
- Evaluate spending practices.
- Determine if the budget is on target with actual performance month to month, expense to expense.
- Establish new goals and objectives for income and spending, as necessary.

Record Keeping is important and you must:

- Be organized.
- Keep good records.
- Maintain an accurate filing system.
- Be able to quickly locate necessary documents.
- Keep all receipts and checks for tax purposes (all receipts and business records should be kept for a period of 7 years as back-up for your tax returns).
- Keep records safe. All important records/ documents should be kept in a fire-proof container, with a professional (i.e., lawyer, accountant), and/or in a safe deposit box.
- Set aside an appropriate time to review and reconcile your monthly statements.

    1. Bank statements
    2. Credit card statements
    3. Investment report statements
    4. Insurance statements, etc.

Notes

Notes

Setting Benchmarks: A guideline to spending

- Set expense benchmarks.
- You must live below your income in order to increase.
- Invest primarily in appreciating assets.
- Don't be house rich and cash poor.
- Don't be car rich and house poor.

Learn to get the best buy - How to maximize your money.

- Use cash or checks, and avoid using credit cards.
- Relate spending to the time required to earn it.
- Understand the value of money in comparison to time.

  Example:
  ($40 dinner at a restaurant or a $40 weekly hairstyle is worth ½ day's wages for a person making $12 per hour)
- Don't buy anything on sale that you would not buy at full price.
- Make sure you absolutely love it and it fits within your budget before purchasing it.
- You must use wisdom in even the small spend ing ventures.

Luke 16:10

10 "He who is faithful in what is least is faithful also in much; and he who is unjust in what is least is unjust also in much. (NKJ)

- It is better to have a few quality items than many poorly-made items.
- Use discounts and coupons.
- Buy in quantity, if possible.
- Look at the price before you look at the product.
- Make sure you understand and calculate the full price (including hidden costs).

Examples:

1. Car (insurance, title fees, taxes, car washes, maintenance, interest payments)
2. House (insurance, maintenance (inside/outside), taxes, landscaping, interest payments)
3. Appliances (maintenance agreements, interest payments, replacement fees, restocking fees on returns)
4. Clothing (dry cleaning, special care requirements)

- Research product and price prior to negotiating.
    a. Check a consumer guide for strengths and weaknesses of the product.
    b. Comparative price shop on the Internet.

5. Get counsel from previous owners and repairmen.

Notes

Workplace Wisdom Institute

Notes

6. Always negotiate price, unless otherwise directed by the Holy Ghost.

Psalm 84:11

11 For the Lord God is a sun and shield; the Lord will give grace and glory; no good thing will He withhold from those who walk uprightly. (NKJ)

Psalm 112:1-7

1 Praise the Lord! Blessed is the man who fears the Lord, who delights greatly in His commandments.
2 His descendants will be mighty on earth; the generation of the upright will be blessed.
3 Wealth and riches will be in his house, and his righteousness endures forever.
4 Unto the upright there arises light in the darkness; he is gracious, and full of compassion, and righteous.
5 A good man deals graciously and lends; he will guide his affairs with discretion.
6 Surely he will never be shaken; the righteous will be in everlasting remembrance.
7 He will not be afraid of evil tidings; his heart is steadfast, trusting in the Lord. (NKJ)

Located in the Budgeting Appendix are forms for personal financial analysis.

a) Personal Financial Statement

b) A Comprehensive Budget Schedule

Module
Study Questions

1. Housing expenses include all of the following except:
   A) Real estate income
   B) Property taxes
   C) Property insurance
   D) Repairs/Maintenance
   E) Electricity

2. Short-term savings is considered an emergency fund and should not be tapped unless absolutely necessary.
   A) True
   B) False

3. All of the following are considered liabilities on your personal financial statement except:
   A) Automobile loan
   B) Real estate
   C) Business loan
   D) Credit card debt

4. "Roll your works upon the Lord, commit and trust them wholly to Him..." is found in:
   A) Luke 14:28
   B) Habakkuk 2:2
   C) Proverbs 16:3 AMP
   D) 1 Corinthians 14:40

5. Ways to get the best buy include all of the following except:
   A) Look at the product before you look at the price.
   B) Use discounts and coupons.
   C) Buy in quantity, if possible.
   D) Make sure you understand and calculate the full price.

6. Planning and preparation are usually not important to success.
   A) True
   B) False

Module
Study Questions, continued

7. The principle found in Genesis 41:34-36 is:
   A) Joseph advised Pharaoh to save 10% of the produce of the land of Egypt.
   B) Joseph advised Pharaoh to save 15% of the produce of the land of Egypt.
   C) Joseph advised Pharaoh to save 20% of the produce of the land of Egypt.
   D) Joseph advised Pharaoh to save 25% of the produce of the land of Egypt.

8. The suggested goal for short-term savings is to have ___ month(s) living expenses saved.
   A) One
   B) Three
   C) Six
   D) Twelve

9. "Let all things be done decently and in order," is found in:
   A) Luke 14:28
   B) Habakkuk 2:2
   C) Proverbs 16:3 AMP
   D) 1 Corinthians 14:40

10. One of the purposes for long-term savings is to provide a godly inheritance for our children and grandchildren.
   A) True
   B) False

11. Record-keeping should include all of the following except:
   A) Organized
   B) Accurate filing system
   C) Record/documents should be kept in a fire proof container.
   D) All receipts and business records can be discarded after a period of three years.

12. It is best not to buy anything on sale that you would not buy at full price.
    A) True
    B) False

13. All of the following are considered assets on your personal financial statement except:
    A) Stocks and bonds
    B) Savings
    C) Home
    D) Home Mortgage

14. Some of the hidden costs of purchasing a house include all of the following except:
    A) Insurance
    B) Replacement fees
    C) Maintenance
    D) Taxes

15. The key to financial increase is to live below your income.
    A) True
    B) False

16. "Write the vision and make it plain on tablets that he may run who reads it," is found in:
    A) Luke 14:28
    B) Habakkuk 2:2
    C) Proverbs 16:3 AMP
    D) 1 Corinthians 14:40

17. Ways to research the product and price prior to negotiating include:
    A) Check consumer guide for strengths and weaknesses of the product.
    B) Comparative price shop on the Internet.
    C) Get counsel from previous owners.
    D) Get counsel from repairmen.
    E) All of the above.

Module
Study Questions, continued

18. When making major purchases, it is not important to calculate all of the hidden costs.
    A) True
    B) False

19. "A good man leaves an inheritance to his children's children," is found in:
    A) Proverbs 13:22
    B) Luke 16:10
    C) Psalm 112:2
    D) Psalm 84:11

20. It is suggested that the average family should live on 70% of their income.
    A) True
    B) False

Budgeting

for

Kingdom Living

Appendix

PERSONAL FINANCIAL STATEMENT

CONFIDENTIAL

Please Print or Type			**If joint statement, complete the following:**	
Name			Name (Spouse)	
Date of Birth	Social Security Number		Date of Birth	Social Security Number
Street Address			Street Address	
City, State, Zip Code			City, State, Zip Code	
Home Phone Number			Home Phone Number	
Present Employer			Present Employer	
Street Address			Street Address	
City, State, Zip Code			City, State. Zip Code	
Position		No. of Years	Position	No. of Years

ESTATE PLANNING INFORMATION

No. of Children/Dependent	Ages	Do you have a will?	If yes, date of will	Name of Personal Representative
Do you have a trust?	If yes, date of trust	Name of Trustee/Successor Trustee		

Cash Income and Expenditures Statement for the Year Ending ____________________

ANNUAL INCOME	AMOUNT	ANNUAL EXPENDITURES	AMOUNT
Salary	$	Property Taxes/Assessments	$
Salary (Spouse)		Income, State, and Other Taxes	
Business & Commissions		Rental Payments	
Dividend Income		Mortgage Payments (Principal & Interest)	
Interest Income		Other Loan Payments	
Rental Income		Contract Payments (Car, Charge Card, etc.)	
Partnership Sub-S Withdrawals (E,F)		Partnership Sub-S Contributions (E,F)	
Capital Gains		Insurance Payments	
Other Investment Income		Alimony, Child Support/Maintenance	
Other Income (List)		Educational Expenses	
		Other Living Expenses	
		Other Expenses	
TOTAL INCOME	$	**TOTAL EXPENDITURES**	$

*All disclosure should be made to reflect income from all sources.

STATEMENT OF ASSETS AND LIABILITIES DATED AS OF ________________________________

*All figures should be in dollars.
*Please attach a separate schedule if more space is needed. Brokerage statements or other such statements may serve in place of required schedule.
*Please use the columns labeled HUSBAND (H) and WIFE (W) for assets owned solely by one or the other and use the JOINT (J) column for all assets owned jointly between the two individuals. If owned jointly with an outside party, please include in the JOINT column, but note with an asterisk. Include all assets held by you as trustee of your living trust in the TRUST (T) column.

ASSETS		H	W	J	T	LIABILITIES	H	W	J	T
Cash Held						Loan Payable Secured				
	Pledged					Loans Payable Unsecured				
	Not Pledged					Other Loans Payable (G)				
Marketable Securities (A)						Accounts & Bills Due				
Accounts & Notes Receivable (B)						Credit Cards Payable				
Net Cash Surrender Value of Life Insurance (c)						Loans against Life Insurance Policy (c)				
Residence						Mortgage Payable Residence				
Other Real Estate (D)						Mortgage Payable - Other Real Estate (D)				
Partnerships Real Estate (E)						Mortgages Payable – Other Real Estate Partnerships				
Other Partnerships – Sub-S Corporation, P.C. (F)						Installation Loans				
IRA, Pension & Profit Sharing						Taxes Payable				
Automobiles						Other Liabilities List				
Personal Property										
Other Assets (List)										
						TOTAL LIABILITIES				
						NET WORTH				
TOTAL ASSETS						**TOTAL**				

Contingent Liabilities for this purpose are defined as obligations that may require payment to be made in the future.

	YES / NO	AMOUNT	LENDER
Are either of you a guarantee, co-maker, or endorser for any debt of an individual, corporation, or partnership?	________	$__________	____________________________
Do you have any outstanding letters of credit or surety bonds?	________	$__________	____________________________
Are you contingently liable on any lease or contract?	________	$__________	____________________________
Are any of your tax obligations past due?	________	$__________	
Any other contingent liabilities that may have a material affect on the information provided?	________	$__________	

If additional detail is needed for any of the items above, please use the space provided below:

SUPPORTING SCHEDULES

SCHEDULE A – MARKETABLE SECURITIES*

No. of Shares (Stock) or Face Value (Bond)	DESCRIPTION	OWNED BY	COST	CURRENT MARKET VALUE	PLEDGED = P RESTRICTED = R
Readily Available Marketable Securities (including U.S. Government and Municipals)					
Other Marketable Securities (Closely held or traded)					

*Brokerage Statement may be included and only totals entered **TOTAL**

SCHEDULE B – ACCOUNTS AND NOTES RECEIVABLE

Name of Debtor	Collateral	Monthly Payment	Maturity Date	Unpaid Balance

SCHEDULE C – LIFE INSURANCE

Name of Insured	Insurance Company	Policy Owner	Beneficiary	Amount	Cash Value	Loans on Policy

SCHEDULE D – REAL ESTATE AND MORTGAGES

Address	Property Type	% Leased	% Owned	Personal Liability	Net Operating Income	Annual Debt Service	Lender	Mortgage Outstand-ing	Market Value

*For additional space, please use the attached page

SCHEDULE E – PARTNERSHIPS (REAL ESTATE)

Partnership Name	Property Location	% Leased	Net Operating Income	Debt Service	% Owned	Personal Liability	Mortgage Outstanding	Market Value	Withdrawals (Contributions)

*For additional space, please use the attached page

SCHEDULE F – OTHER PARTNERSHIPS (NON-REAL ESTATE)

Investment Name	Date of Initial Investment	Investment Amount	% Owned	Mortgage Outstanding	Market Value	Withdrawals (Contributions)

SCHEDULE G – OTHER LOANS PAYABLE

To Whom	Address	Name of Debtor	Collateral	Interest Rate	Maturity Date	Monthly Payment	Unpaid Balance

Please Check ( ) if additional forms are included.

Have (either of) you or any company in which (either of) you were a major owner ever declared bankruptcy in the last seven years? /_/Yes /_/No

Have (either of) you ever had a judgment against you? /_/Yes /_/No

Are any assets pledged or debts secured, except as shown? If yes, please indicate on a separate sheet which assets and their value. /_/Yes /_/No

Are (either of) you a defendant in any suits or legal action? /_/Yes /_/No

Have any of your tax returns been audited or contested? /_/Yes /_/No

Do (either of) you have a line of credit at any other financial institution? If yes, please indicate the institution, the amount, and the name of your Account Office. /_/Yes /_/No

If you have answered "yes" to any of the above questions, please explain in the space provided below or on a separate sheet. /_/Yes /_/No

NOTES:

DOMINATING MONEY
PERSONAL FINANCIAL STATEMENT

ASSETS (Present Market Value)

Cash on hand/checking account	$
Cash Held/Savings	$
Stocks and bonds	$
Cash value of life insurance	$
Coins	$
Personal Residence	$
Other real estate	$
Mortgages/notes receivable	$
Automobiles	$
Furniture	$
Jewelry	$
Other Personal Property	$
Business Valuations	$
Other Partnership	$
IRA/Pension/Retirement plan	$
Other Assets	$
Total Assets	$

LIABILITIES (Current Amount Owed)

Accounts and Current Bills	$
Credit Cards Payable	$
Automobile Loans	$
Residence Mortgage	$
Other Real Estate Mortgages	$
Installation Loans	$
Outstanding Medical Bills	$
Life Insurance Loans	$
Business/Partnership Loans	$
Personal Debts to Relatives	$
Other Liabilities	$
Taxes Payable	$
Total Liabilities	$

NET WORTH (Total assets minus total liabilities)

Net Worth	$

BUDGET (Page 1)

NET WAGES / INCOME

Gross Income, Wages $ ____________________

Federal Income Tax $__________________

State and City Income Tax $__________________

Social Security Tax $__________________

Other Deductions $__________________

Total Tax & Deductions $__________________

Net Income, Wages $____________________

INCOME

	Monthly	Annual
Net Income, Wages	$	$
Interest, Dividends	$	$
Net Rent Income	$	$
Net Business Income	$	$
Retirement Income	$	$
Other Income	$	$

Total Annual Income $____________

Total Monthly Income $____________

Divide annual income by 12 to get monthly income

DEBT REPAYMENT

	Monthly	Annual
Total from Debt List	$	$

Total Annual Debt $____________

Total Monthly Debt $____________

Divide annual debt by 12 to get monthly debt

CHILD CARE

	Monthly	Annual
Educational Expenses / Tuition	$	$
Tutoring	$	$
Allowances	$	$
Music/Dance/Other Lessons	$	$
Sports	$	$
Latchkey / Babysitting	$	$
Other	$	$

Total Annual Child Care Costs $____________

Total Monthly Child Care Costs $____________

Divide annual childcare costs by 12 to get monthly childcare costs

BUDGET (Page 2)

FOOD

	Monthly	Annual
Groceries	$	$
Dining Out	$	$
School Lunches	$	$
Other	$	$

Total Annual Food $______________

Total Monthly Food $______________

Divide annual food bill by 12 to get monthly food bill

CLOTHING/GROOMING

	Monthly	Annual
Purchases	$	$
Cleaning	$	$
Hair / Nail Care	$	$
Toiletries	$	$

Total Annual Clothing $______________

Total Monthly Clothing $______________

Divide annual clothing bill by 12 to get monthly clothing bill

HOUSEHOLD

	Monthly	Annual
Rent/Mortgage	$	$
Property Taxes	$	$
Property Insurance	$	$
Electricity	$	$
Heating/Gas	$	$
Water	$	$
Garbage Removal	$	$
Satellite /Cable TV	$	$
Telephone/Cellular/Pager	$	$
Professional Cleaning	$	$
Repairs/Maintenance	$	$
Household Supplies	$	$
Improvements	$	$
Furnishings	$	$
Other	$	$

Total Annual Household Costs $______________

Total Monthly Household Costs $______________

Divide annual household costs by 12 to get monthly household costs

BUDGET (Page 3)

TRANSPORTATION

	Monthly	Annual
Gas	$	$
Automobile/Boat/RV Insurance	$	$
Repair/Maintenance/Storage	$	$
Licenses/Registration	$	$
Parking/Tolls/Mass Transit	$	$

Total Annual Transportation $__________

Total Monthly Transportation $__________

Divide annual transportation by 12 to get monthly transportation

MEDICAL / DENTAL

	Monthly	Annual
Medical	$	$
Dental	$	$
Optical	$	$
Prescriptions	$	$
Health Insurance	$	$
Other	$	$

Total Annual Medical/Dental $__________

Total Monthly Medical/Dental $__________

Divide annual medical/dental by 12 to get monthly medical/dental

INSURANCE

	Monthly	Annual
Life Insurance	$	$
Disability	$	$
Other	$	$

Total Annual Insurance $__________

Total Monthly Insurance $__________

Divide annual insurance by 12 to get monthly insurance

ENTERTAINMENT

	Monthly	Annual
Entertainment/Theatre/Sports Events	$	$
Vacations	$	$
Hobbies	$	$
CDs/Tapes/Videos	$	$
Books/Magazines/Newspaper	$	$
Pets	$	$

Total Annual Entertainment $__________

Total Monthly Entertainment $__________

Divide annual entertainment by 12 to get monthly entertainment

BUDGET (Page 4)

PERSONAL BUSINESS

	Monthly	Annual
Education	$	$
Clubs/Unions/Dues	$	$
Accounting/Legal	$	$
Financial Services	$	$
Other	$	$

Total Annual Personal Business $______________

Total Monthly Personal Business $______________

Divide annual personal business by 12 to get monthly personal business

DONATIONS

	Monthly	Annual
Church	$	$
Other Ministries	$	$
Charities	$	$

Total Annual Donations $______________

Total Monthly Donations $______________

Divide annual donations by 12 to get monthly donations

SAVINGS

	Monthly	Annual
Emergency Savings	$	$
Permanent Savings	$	$
Retirement Savings	$	$

Total Annual Savings $______________

Total Monthly Savings $______________

Divide annual savings by 12 to get monthly savings

GIFTS

	Monthly	Annual
Christmas	$	$
Birthdays/Anniversaries	$	$
Weddings/Showers	$	$
Graduations	$	$
Office Gifts	$	$

Total Annual Gifts $______________

Total Monthly Gifts $______________

Divide annual gifts by 12 to get monthly gifts

TOTALS

TOTAL INCOME $ ____________________

TOTAL EXPENSES $ ____________________ **SURPLUS OR DEFICIT** $ ____________________

RECORDING YOUR INCOME AND SPENDING

Date					
Mo.	Day	Description	Method of Spending	Amount of Spending	Amount of Income

Notes

Eliminating Debt

Eliminating Debt

Debt often strikes us as a bad word. It conjures up feelings of remorse. Depending upon where we are in the debt spectrum, it can be a real source of anguish, frustration, and pain. In fact, some Christians have committed suicide due to overwhelming debt obligations. None of this is in any way godly! Yet, many Christians are fraught with debt. Debt freedom is God's best, and He desires that the body of Christ move towards a debt-free state of mind and reality.

Debt is a way of life in the United States of America. According to Cardweb.com, "Bank credit card loans in the U.S. totaled $568.4 billion in 2000, up 16.0 percent from the 1999 figure of $490.1 billion. During 2000, Americans charged more than $1.2 trillion on their VISA, Mastercard, Discover, and American Express cards." Based on a report issued by the Federal Reserve, "At the end of February 2002, American consumers were $1.669 trillion in debt, exclusive of home mortgages."

This chapter discusses:

- What the scriptures say about debt.
- How people get into debt.
- How to eliminate debt.

It is designed to give the Christian God's perspective toward debt and provide meaningful and practical methods for eliminating debt.

Workplace Wisdom Institute

Debt

Notes

Definition of debt:

Money, property, or services which one person has obligated himself to pay another.

Debt includes:

- Money owed to credit companies
- Bank loans
- Department store credit cards or financing
- Money borrowed from relatives, friends, and others
- Home mortgages
- Home Equity Loans
- Auto loans
- Past Due Bills

Definition of credit:

A pledge to pay in the future for what is received in the present.

Definition of interest:

The fee charged by the creditor for the use of money or for borrowing money.

"The use of credit essentially means we are using a portion of tomorrow's income to pay more than something is worth so we can have it today!!"
Ray Linder

Notes

Business Debt

- In 1999, U.S. non-financial corporations owed $4.2 trillion dollars in debt. (According to the "Philadelphia Trumpet," page 4, March/April 2000.)
- In 1960, corporations paid $7.6 billion dollars in interest. In 1990, corporations paid $200 billion dollars in interest.
- In 1990, 51% of all corporate profits were being eaten up by interest.

Total Consumer Debt:

According to derekcrane.com/facts:

1992: $782.2 billion 2000: $1,509.5 billion

Americans paid out approximately $65 billion in interest in 2001, alone.

Personal Debt

- In 1990, individuals owed more than three trillion dollars in debt.

According to the "Philadelphia Trumpet," page 4, March/April 2000:

- In 1999, individuals owed $6.3 trillion dollars in debt.
- In 1999, individuals owed $1.4 trillion dollars in credit debt.
- In 1990, 23% of the average person's take-home pay was committed to the payment of existing debt (not including the home mortgage).

Eliminating Debt

- In 2001, more than 1.4 million individuals filed bankruptcy, the highest in American history. (Source: Abiworld.org/stats)
- In 1990, a Gallup Poll found that 56% of all divorces are a result of financial tension in the home.
- The average American credit card balance is $7,000, and the average interest rates 18.9% per Consumercredit.com.

Notes

Luke 16:10-11

10 He who is faithful in what is least is faithful also in much; and he who is unjust in what is least is unjust also in much.
11 Therefore if you have not been faithful in the unrighteous mammon, who will commit to your trust the true riches? (NKJ)

Workplace Wisdom Institute

Notes

What the Scriptures Say About Debt

God's Word does not overly prohibit or forbid borrowing or accumulating debt. Neither is debt considered a sin. However, the Bible clearly warns about the destructive power of debt.

Debt is not God's best.

1. **Debt is considered a curse.**

   - The Old Testament regards debt as a curse.
   - Debt is not a sin. However, it is not God's best for Christians to get into debt.
   - Debt was used in the Old Testament as a means of preventing financial ruin.

Deuteronomy 28:1-2, 12

1 Now it shall come to pass, if you diligently obey the voice of the Lord your God, to observe carefully all His commandments which I command you today, that the Lord your God will set you high above all nations of the earth.
2 And all these blessings shall come upon you and overtake you, because you obey the voice of the Lord your God:
12 The Lord will open to you His good treasure, the heavens, to give the rain to your land in its season, and to bless all the work of your hand. You shall lend to many nations, but you shall not borrow. (NKJ)

Deuteronomy 28:15, 43-44

15 But it shall come to pass, if you do not obey the voice of the Lord your God, to observe carefully all His commandments and His statutes which I command you today, that all these **curses** will come upon you and overtake you:
43 The alien who is among you shall rise higher

and higher above you, and you shall come down
lower and lower.
44 He shall lend to you, but you shall not lend to
him; he shall be the head, and you shall be the
tail. (NKJ)

2. Debt is considered slavery. It produces bondage to creditors.

Proverbs 22:7

7 The rich rules over the poor, and the borrower
is servant to the lender. (NKJ)

3. Debt presumes upon the future.

Borrowing assumes the individual will have the financial resources to pay the loan back in the future. This is often not the case.

Fundamental Truth

According to Consumercredit.com, almost half of the households in America report having difficulty paying their minimum monthly payments.

James 4:13-15

13 Come now, you who say, "Today or tomorrow
we will go to such and such a city, spend a year
there, buy and sell, and make a profit";
14 whereas you do not know what will happen
tomorrow. For what is your life? It is even a vapor
that appears for a little time and then vanishes
away.
15 Instead you ought to say, "If the Lord wills, we
shall live and do this or that." (NKJ)

Proverbs 27:1

1 Do not boast about tomorrow, for you do not
know what a day may bring forth. (NKJ)

Notes

Notes

What the Scriptures Say About Debt
continued

4. **Debt removes barriers to harmful issues.**

   - There are instances when God may have not manifest money because it may be the wrong item or the wrong timing. Borrowing can prematurely bring possessions into a person's life or against God's will.

James 4:3

3 You ask and do not receive, because you ask amiss, that you may spend it on your pleasures. (NKJ)

1 Timothy 6:9

9 But those who desire to be rich fall into temptation and a snare, and into many foolish and harmful lusts which drown men in destruction and perdition. (NKJ)

5. **Debt projects the illusion of independence from God and can interfere with His provisions.**

   - Borrowing can encourage financial decisions to be made independently of God's provisions.

   - Premature financial decisions can be made when loans are available, interfering with the manifestation of God's supernatural provision in a person's life.

Notes

James 4:13-15

13 Come now, you who say, "Today or tomorrow we will go to such and such a city, spend a year there, buy and sell, and make a profit";
14 whereas you do not know what will happen tomorrow. For what is your life? It is even a vapor that appears for a little time and then vanishes away.
15 Instead you ought to say, "If the Lord wills, we shall live and do this or that." (NKJ)

Psalm 37:23

23 The steps of a good man are ordered by the LORD, and He delights in his way. (NKJ)

Ecclesiastes 5:10

10 He who loves silver will not be satisfied with silver; nor he who loves abundance, with increase. This also is vanity. (NKJ)

6. **Debt promotes impulse buying and causes overspending.**

7. **Debt devours resources through high interest payments.**

   - Creditors make a profit by loaning money and charging interest, which can be excessive.
   - Interest payments will reduce the financial resources that are available for the individual to use.

Notes

Interest payments are a deadly trap for the borrower. Most people fail to understand the final price tag of borrowing someone else's money if they do not have the capacity to easily repay.

Amortization Schedule

Principle balance after down payment - $100,000
Interest rate - 7.5%
Mortgage length - 30 years
Monthly payment - $699.21

Payment #	Month	Payment	Interest	Principal Paid	Principal Balance
1	Jan	699.21	625.00	74.21	99,925.79
2	Feb	699.21	624.54	74.68	99,851.11
3	Mar	699.21	624.07	75.15	99,775.96
4	Apr	699.21	623.60	75.61	99,700.35
5	May	699.21	623.13	76.09	99,624.26
6	June	699.21	622.65	76.56	99,547.70
7	July	699.21	622.17	77.04	99,470.66
8	Aug	699.21	621.69	77.52	99,393.13
9	Sep	699.21	621.21	78.01	99,315.13
10	Oct	699.21	620.72	78.49	99,236.63
11	Nov	699.21	620.23	78.99	99,157.64
12	Dec	699.21	619.74	79.48	99,078.17
	Total	8390.57	7468.74	921.83	

30 Year Mortgage Payments

Principle Balance after down payment - $100,000

Interest Rate	Amount Borrowed	Monthly Payment	Monthly Interest	Total Interest Paid	Total Payments
6.5	100,000	632.07	354.29	127,544.49	227,544.49
7.0	100,000	665.30	387.52	139,508.90	239,508.90
7.5	100,000	699.21	421.44	151,717.22	251,717.22
8.0	100,000	733.76	455.99	164,155.25	264,155.25
8.5	100,000	768.91	491.14	176,808.85	276,808.85
9.0	100,000	804.62	526.84	189,664.14	289,664.14
9.5	100,000	840.85	563.08	202,707.51	302,707.51
10.0	100,000	877.57	599.79	215,925.77	315,925.77

When financial resources are monopolized through debt repayment, it prevents the believer from being able to freely give to support and further the Gospel or be a blessing to others.

The Law of Compounded Interest

How much money does the average person make from age 25 to 65 (in 40 years)?

40 years of compounded interest at 7% yields substantial rewards.

Salary/ Year $	40 years total earned (No raises or interest earned or other source of income)	20% of gross wages saved/year	20% saved at 7% interest rate for 40 years
$15,000	$600,000	$3,000	$643,828
$20,000	$800,000	$4,000	$858,438
$25,000	$1,000,000	$5,000	$1,073,048
$30,000	$1,200,000	$6,000	$1,287,657
$40,000	$1,600,000	$8,000	$1,716,877
$50,000	$2,000,000	$10,000	$2,146,096
$75,000	$3,000,000	$15,000	$3,219,145
$100,000	$4,000,000	$20,000	$4,292,191

Workplace Wisdom Institute

Notes

How People Get Into Debt

1. Over-use of credit cards
2. Living above their means
3. Personal Indulgence- the "I deserve it," syndrome
4. Acquiring status symbols, maintaining images, and perpetuating lifestyles
5. Being financially unprepared for emergencies and crises – No savings
6. Not properly managing not budgeting
7. Denial
   - Not opening bills
   - Not knowing how much is actually owed
   - The "What difference does it make?" syndrome
8. Poor business decisions
9. Pledging personal assets for business
10. Co-signing - surety

Surety

Notes

Definition of Surety:

A person who agrees to be legally responsible for the debt or default of another.

In 1990, 50% of those who co-signed for bank loans ended up making the payments.

In 1990, 75% of those who co-signed for finance company loans ended up making the payments.

Proverbs 22:26-27

26 Do not be one of those who shakes hands in a
pledge, one of those who is surety for debts;
27 If you have nothing with which to pay, why
should he take away your bed from under you?
(NKJ)

Proverbs 17:18

18 A man devoid of understanding shakes hands in a pledge, and becomes surety for his friend. (NKJ)

Proverbs 11:15

15 He who is surety for a stranger will suffer, but one who hates being surety is secure. (NKJ)

Proverbs 6:1-5

1 My son, if you become surety for your friend, if
you have shaken hands in pledge for a stranger,
2 You are snared by the words of your mouth;
you are taken by the words of your mouth.
3 So do this, my son, and deliver yourself; for you
have come into the hand of your friend: go and
humble yourself; plead with your friend.
4 Give no sleep to your eyes, nor slumber to your
eyelids.
5 Deliver yourself like a gazelle from the hand of
the hunter, and like a bird from the hand of the
fowler. (NKJ)

Notes

The Advantages of Being Debt Free

1. The freedom to have financial pressures, anxiety and strain minimized and manageable
2. The freedom to think and dream about one's financial future
3. The freedom and luxury to give to God and others
4. The freedom to make wise and godly financial decisions
5. The freedom to walk in God's peace
6. The freedom to take advantage of sound investment opportunities
7. The freedom to save and plan for future needs

"God's work done in God's way will not lack God's support. He is just as able to supply the funds ahead of time as afterward and he much prefers doing so." J. Hudson Taylor

How to Eliminate Debt

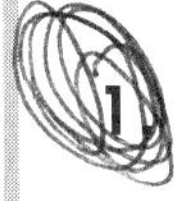

1. **Pray and fast for wisdom on how to manage money.**

James 1:5

5 If any of you lacks wisdom, let him ask of God, who gives to all liberally and without reproach, and it will be given to him. (NKJ)

Proverbs 2:6-7

6 For the LORD gives wisdom; from His mouth come knowledge and understanding;
7 He stores up sound wisdom for the upright; he is a shield to those who walk uprightly; (NKJ)

Wisdom Point
The effective management and stewardship of money and resources is vitally important to the elimination of debt.

2. **List your liabilities (everything you owe) on the Debt Repayment Schedule, and determine your debt/income ratio.**

   a. Debt column - List the name of the debt and the company to which the debt is owed (e.g., home mortgage - Comerica Bank, minivan - Ford Motor Credit Company, Visa - Bank One).

   b. Total Balance column - List the remaining outstanding balance due to completely pay off the loan.

   c. Monthly Payments column - List the minimum monthly payment required to pay the loan.

   d. Interest Rate column - List the loan's interest rate.

Notes

How to Eliminate Debt, continued

2. **List your liabilities (everything you owe) on the Debt Repayment Schedule, and determine your Debt/Income Ratio**

   e. Payments Past Due column - Add the total amount of payments that are past due and list in this column.

   f. Debt/Income Ratio column - List the total monthly mortgage payment and total monthly payments of all outstanding debts, and place in the total monthly debt column. *Calculate family monthly gross income; that is, the total income prior to any deductions (taxes, retirement, etc.). Divide the total monthly debt by the total gross income, and then multiply by 100 to obtain debt-to-income ratio.

Note: The remainder of the debt repayment schedule will be completed in another section.

*Do not include monthly expenses such as utilities, groceries, tuition, car insurance, etc.

Example:

House payment (principal, interest, property taxes). . .	$965
Car payments(2) . . .	540
VISA. . .	45
Mastercard . . .	65
Retail card . . .	22
Home equity loan . . .	115
	$1,752 /
Total gross monthly income	4,250 =
	.41X 100
	= **41%**

Formula: Debt/Income Ratio
Total monthly debt/Total gross income X 100

Workplace Wisdom Institute

Debt/Income Ratio	
Debt as % of income	Evaluation
Less than 30%	Acceptable
31% — 35%	Fair
35% — 50%	Problematic
Greater than 50%	Debt out of control

Notes

3. **List all assets (everything that is stewarded or "owned") on Asset Schedule.**

   a. Asset Description column - List the type of asset in groups and name (e.g. vacation property - Orlando timeshare, real estate investment - 925 Indiana duplex, stocks - Wal-Mart, mutual fund - Fidelity Growth Fund, auto - minivan, jewelry - Movado watch, power tools - table saw, electronics - big-screen TV).

   b. Current Value column - List the current value of the asset.

   c. Balance Due column - List the balance that is due to completely pay off the loan.

   d. Net After Sale column - List the final amount to be received after the sale has been completed and the expenses paid, including loan repayments, commissions, taxes, etc.

Notes

How to Eliminate Debt, continued

3. List all assets (everything that is stewarded or "owned") on the Assets Schedule

e. Monthly Expenses column - List the monthly expenses that are necessary to maintain the item; include monthly loan payments, monthly maintenance, estimate monthly taxes and insurance.

f. Need Index column - List the need index or priority.

Priority Code A - High priority to maintain, should be maintained, if possible at all costs, asset is the proper size and value, does not need to be downsized or sold.

Priority Code B - Medium priority to maintain, attempt to maintain if possible, may need to downsize, exchange or be sold.

Priority Code C - Low priority to maintain, not absolutely necessary for survival, possibly needs to be sold.

Priority Code D -Very low priority, absolutely not necessary, needs to be sold.

g. Should it be sold? column - Answer yes or no, and be honest and commit to the answer.

Notes

4. **Sell assets that are not absolutely necessary.**

- Cars
- Golf clubs
- Jewelry
- Vacation homes
- Collections
- Furs
- Investments (stocks, bonds, etc.)
- Real Estate
- Retirement plan assets
- Power tools
- Appliances
- Electronics
- Furniture
- Recreational vehicles
- Have a garage sale

5. **Lower your standard of living**

- Downsize house (apartment living)
- Downsize car
- Reduce tuition payments
- Reduce vacations and entertainment expenses

Notes

How to Eliminate Debt, continued

- Reduce eating expenses – fast food, cook instead of eating out, use coupons, cook fresh foods
- Reduce clothing expenses – shop in your closet, shop in thrift stores, learn to sew, wear hand-me-downs, avoid designer clothes and other expensive clothes

6. **Establish a written budget, and follow it.**

   If necessary, use professional credit counseling

   A. Consumer Credit Corporation (CCCS)
   8611 Second Avenue
   Suite 100
   Silver Spring, MD 20910
   800-388-2227

   B. Christian Credit Counselors, Inc.
   800-305-3528

7. **Stop spending more than you currently earn, and create a Debt Eliminator.**

   A. Reduce your spending by approximately 10% of your monthly gross income.

   B. Use this 10% (Debt Eliminator) on a monthly basis to eliminate your debt. If your monthly gross income is $2,000, then you should reduce your expenditures to save $200 per month. This $200 per month (Debt Eliminator) should then be added to the minimum payments required to reduce your debt.

Once the debt is completely eliminated, apply this entire amount to the next debt, along with its monthly payment to speed up the payoff process.

Notes

Ways to reduce spending:

- Buy generic products rather than brand-name products.
- Don't buy anything new that you can buy used.
- Be a bargain hunter.
- Use cash or checks rather than credit cards.
- Avoid extended warranties for appliances.
- Shop early for gifts in order to find bargains.
- Shop at thrift and discount stores.
- Always use a shopping list and avoid purchasing things that are not on the list.
- Never shop when hungry or depressed; you will have the tendency to purchase more than you need or things you don't need.
- Use discount coupons and certificates.
- Mail in the rebate coupons.
- Minimize the purchase of extra features and services.

Notes

How to Eliminate Debt, continued

Ways to reduce spending:

- Purchase items from garage sales, public auctions, and flea markets.
- Donate unused items to your church or charity for a tax deduction.
- Purchase an excellent used car rather than a new car.
- Purchase mildly damaged furniture, appli ances and clothes at tremendous discounts.
- Always negiotiate the price unless directed by the Holy Ghost not to.
- Avoid purchasing unnecessary and expensive exercise equipment until you have determined that the exercise is a fixed habit.
- Avoid leasing cars.
- Start car pooling.
- Avoid speeding and parking tickets.
- Raise insurance deductibles.
- Save on your energy bills: use dishwasher less, use energy-efficient appliances, turn down the thermostat, use ceiling fans, insulate all doors and windows, use electric blankets, fix leaky faucets, use low-flow shower heads, water grass in the morning, don't waste water, hang clothes out to dry, use cold water to wash clothes.

- Minimize long distance calling by using e-mail.
- Get the basic phone package, and discontinue the extra phone service options.
- Shop your long distance carrier to get the best rates.
- Minimize your cellular phone expenses by talking less or using a pager.
- Perform your own home repairs, carpet cleaning, and new paint jobs.
- Use rechargeable batteries.
- Use hand towels rather than paper towels and napkins
- Wash and reuse plastic food storage bags and aluminum foil.
- Shop for discount pet food and supplies.
- Make your own baby food.
- Make your own lunch rather than eating out.
- Buy items in bulk.
- Use a water filter rather than buying bottled water.

Note: Do not get discouraged if you cannot reduce your monthly expenses by 10% to establish the Debt Eliminator. If necessary, start with 5% or even 2% and then build a larger Debt Eliminator as you pay off debt and more funds become available.

Notes

Notes

How to Eliminate Debt, continued

8. **Establish a debt repayment schedule for every creditor on the Debt Repayment Schedule.**

   a. Pay off Priority column - Determine which loans should be paid off first, rank 1-100 with 1 being the first loan to be paid off.

      - First pay off past-due balances, if possible.
      - Pay small debts early to gain confidence.
      - Pay off higher interest rates quickly.

   b. Monthly Payment with Eliminator column - Add the Debt Eliminator (10% of monthly gross income) to the minimum monthly payment. When the first debt has been paid off, add its monthly payment and the Debt Eliminator to the minimum payment of the second debt; continue this process until all the debts have been paid off.

   c. Avoid debt consolidation (unless you close charge accounts).

Wisdom Point
A Christian should not choose bankruptcy as an option.

Notes

Exodus 20:15

15 You shall not steal. (NKJ)

Psalm 37:21

21 The wicked borrows and does not repay, but the righteous shows mercy and gives. (NKJ)

When debts are not repaid, it is a violation of scripture. One of the Ten Commandments states, "You shall not steal." When a debt is not repaid, it is stealing. The money does not belong to the borrower. It belongs to the creditor and has never been returned. There was a pledge to return the money, and the pledge was broken. This is why Psalm 37 refers to the person who does not repay a loan as "wicked."

Christians should never choose to operate in wickedness. They should walk in righteousness. A righteous person does not steal from others, but repays debts.

Even if an individual is forced into a legal bankruptcy, they are not released from the moral and spiritual principles related to repaying the loan. A truly righteous person would attempt to repay as much of the debt as possible over the years, even if they have been legally released from the debt.

Many individuals have been legally released from debt through a personal bankruptcy. Years later they received a windfall of money and returned to pay off old obligations prior to using the money to prosper.

9. Do not accumulate any more debt.

- Use cash, checks, or debit cards.
- Cut up credit cards.
- Close credit accounts by sending a letter to the company requesting its closure.

Notes

How to Eliminate Debt, continued

9. Do not accumulate any more debt.

- If you must use a credit card, pay off the total balance when the bill is due.
- Budget your money wisely.

Borrowing considerations

Debt should be avoided if at all possible. However, debt should only be utilized when there is economic justification for it. Good debts have the future ability to recover the additional cost of credit (recapture through asset appreciation).

- Houses and real estate - The early payoff of houses and real estate can sometimes recapture the additional cost of the interest payments by the appreciation of the asset.
- Business investments - Sound business investments with good cash flow and appreciation of the asset can sometimes justify the additional cost of the interest payments. Wisdom and caution, however, must be utilized. Many people have lost money through unwise business dealings and "get-rich-quick" schemes, causing major financial difficulties.
- Cars - The use of a modest car to aid and assist in producing income (going to and from work) can sometimes justify the additional cost of the interest pay-

ments. However, cars are depreciable assets.

Wisdom must be used not to purchase with credit more car than is absolutely necessary. Used cars, one to two years old, are excellent buys because the initial depreciation has already been adjusted.

- Education - The future earnings potential of an educated person can sometimes justify the additional cost of interest payments. However, be very cautious; student loans have caused many people financial difficulty over the years.

Notes

Wisdom Point
Debt should never be used to purchase luxury or non-essential items.

Most people get into financial trouble using debt to purchase items they cannot yet afford. If they would wait patiently until the money is manifested, financial burdens and frustrations could be reduced.

Avoid using credit to purchase depreciable or consumable items.

- Clothes
- Jewelry
- Retail purchases
- Furniture and fixtures
- Travel and vacations
- Home appliances and electronics

Notes

How to Eliminate Debt, continued

- Home decorations
- Groceries
- Any other depreciating items

Borrowing money to purchase these items is a poor use of credit because the additional cost of interest cannot be recovered. It is poor stewardship of God's money. Wait until you have accumulated the appropriate amount of cash before purchasing these items.

If credit is absolutely necessary to purchase durable goods, such as furniture and major household appliances, purpose to pay off the debt in three to six months or sooner.

Note: We are not saying that it is a sin to borrow money or that it should never be done. However, it should be avoided, if possible. When borrowing money becomes absolutely necessary, do not allow yourself to live with the loan to its full term. Make every effort to pay off the loan as quickly as possible.

10. Earn additional income.

One of the most important ways to eliminate debt is to ask God for creativity to increase cash flow. This requires diligence and an excellent work ethic. It is not only important for eliminating debt and meeting financial obligations, but is also a very important key to financial prosperity.

Eliminating Debt

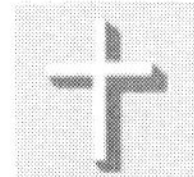

Proverbs 10:4
4 He who has a slack hand becomes poor, but the hand of the diligent makes rich. (NKJ)

The way to eliminate debt is to spend less than you earn and use the surplus to pay off your debts. This is accomplished by two methods. The first one is to develop a good budget and reduce your spending habits. The second method is to increase the money you earn.

Ways to earn more money

- Perform your current job with such excellence that you deserve a raise or increased commissions.
- Work overtime.
- Get a temporary second job.
- Have teenagers work.
- Start a home-based business.
- Develop creative business ideas.

Creative business ideas

- Crafts and designs
- Babysitting, day care, or nanny services
- Landscaping, shoveling snow
- Housekeeping
- Inventions
- Computer work, graphics, and word processing

Notes

Workplace Wisdom Institute

Notes

How to Eliminate Debt, continued

Creative business ideas

- Knitting
- Flower arrangements
- Desktop publishing
- Resume service
- Nail service
- Cooking classes
- Wallpapering service
- Home repair service
- Mail-order business
- Car washing and detailing
- Portrait artist
- Personalize story books
- Web site design
- Instructional design
- Second-hand clothing
- Online sportswear
- Embroidery service
- Seamstress
- Formal wear rentals
- Linen supply service
- Custom necktie sales
- Mystery dinner parties
- Satellite dish sales and installation
- Tax preparation
- Bookkeeping service
- Image consultant
- Employee training
- Headhunter service
- Jingle writer
- Fundraising consultant
- Seminar speaker
- Pre-packaged nutritional food sales
- Luncheon/dinner sandwich delivery route
- Juice bar sales
- Catering service
- Dessert shop
- Skin care product sales
- Maid service
- Carpet cleaning
- Training services

- Dry-cleaning service
- Mobile office service
- Computer repair
- Medical billing service
- On-line tour service
- Used computer sales
- Career expos
- Inventory service
- Online researcher

11. Be content with what you have.

1 Timothy 6:6-11

6 Now godliness with contentment is great gain.
7 For we brought nothing into this world, and it is
certain we can carry nothing out.
8 And having food and clothing, with these we
shall be content.
9 But those who desire to be rich fall into temptation and a snare, and into many foolish and
harmful lusts which drown men in destruction and
perdition.
10 For the love of money is a root of all kinds of
evil, for which some have strayed from the faith in
their greediness, and pierced themselves through
with many sorrows.
11 But you, O man of God, flee these things and
pursue righteousness, godliness, faith, love, patience, gentleness. (NKJ)

Notes

How to Eliminate Debt, continued

Operating in the character qualities of contentment and patience is important for eliminating debt and preventing future over expenditures.

12. Do not give up while eliminating debt. Remember, it takes time and effort.

Sometimes it's easier to give up rather than persevere in eliminating debt. Do not allow yourself to become discouraged. God has blessed you with the strength and ability to completely eliminate debt.

Philippians 4: 13

13 I can do all things through Christ who strengthens me. (NKJ)

Not

Supernatural Debt Cancellation

The widow's oil

II Kings 4: 1-7

1 A certain woman of the wives of the sons o
the prophets cried out to Elisha, saying, "Your
servant my husband is dead, and you know that
your servant feared the LORD. And the creditor is
coming to take my two sons to be his slaves."
2 So Elisha said to her, "What shall I do for you?
Tell me, what do you have in the house?" And
she said, "Your maidservant has nothing in the
house but a jar of oil."
3 Then he said, "Go, borrow vessels from everywhere, from all your neighbors—empty vessels;
do not gather just a few.
4 "And when you have come in, you shall shut
the door behind you and your sons; then pour it
into all those vessels, and set aside the full ones."
5 So she went from him and shut the door behind
her and her sons, who brought the vessels to her;
and she poured it out.
6 Now it came to pass, when the vessels were
full, that she said to her son, "Bring me another
vessel." And he said to her, "There is not another
vessel." So the oil ceased.
7 Then she came and told the man of God. And
he said, "Go, sell the oil and pay your debt; and
you and your sons live on the rest."
(NKJ)

- God gave the widow a business plan. He anointed the plan, and then required that she work the plan in order for its fulfillment to be manifested in her life.
- God told her what business to develop, where to get the resources, what to sell, and what to do with the profits of the business.

Workplace Wisdom Institute

Supernatural Debt Cancellation, continued

- God anointed and multiplied what she already had in her house to deliver her from financial bondage (vs. 2).
- God required that she go to the community, her neighbors, and persuade them to assist her in developing an infrastructure for her business (vs. 3).
- The sons of the widow, her entire family, worked in the development of the business (vs. 5).
- God only filled to capacity and stopped the multiplication at the level to which she had previously prepared. He only supplied the resources which her stewardship could manage (vs. 6).
- God required that she sell the oil and work in order to pay the debts (vs. 7).
- God provided not only the cancellation of her debts in her new found business, but He also provided through the business the ability for the woman to meet her future financial obligations (vs. 7).
- This is not just an example of supernatural debt cancellation; it is also an example of financial increase and prosperity, because the widow's future financial needs were also addressed. She had more than enough (vs. 7).
- Because the widow was obedient and operated on the Word of God that came to her, she was able to get her financial breakthrough.

Workplace Wisdom Institute

What to Do as You Get Out of Debt

Notes

Don't Worry

Philippians 4:6-8

6 Be anxious for nothing, but in everything by
prayer and supplication, with thanksgiving, let
your requests be made known to God;
7 and the peace of God, which surpasses all
understanding, will guard your hearts and minds
through Christ Jesus.
8 Finally, brethren, whatever things are true,
whatever things are noble, whatever things are
just, whatever things are pure, whatever things
are lovely, whatever things are of good report, if
there is any virtue and if there is anything praise-
worthy—meditate on these things. (NKJ)

1 Peter 5:7

7 casting all your care upon Him, for He cares for you. (NKJ)

Go to Church

Psalm 133:1-3

1 Behold, how good and how pleasant it is for
brethren to dwell together in unity!
2 It is like the precious oil upon the head, running
down on the beard, the beard of Aaron, running
down on the edge of his garments.
3 It is like the dew of Hermon, descending upon
the mountains of Zion; for there the Lord commanded the blessing—life forevermore. (NKJ)

Hebrews 10:25

25 not forsaking the assembling of ourselves together, as is the manner of some, but exhorting one another, and so much the more as you see the Day approaching. (NKJ)

Notes

What to Do as You Get Out of Debt, continued

Continue Giving

Galatians 6:9

9 And let us not grow weary while doing good, for in due season we shall reap if we do not lose heart. (NKJ)

Pray and Praise God

Psalm 34:1,3,4,6-8,19

1 I will bless the Lord at all times; his praise shall continually be in my mouth.
3 Oh, magnify the Lord with me, and let us exalt His name together.
4 I sought the Lord, and He heard me, and delivered me from all my fears.
6 This poor man cried out, and the Lord heard him, and saved him out of all his troubles.
7 The angel of the Lord encamps all around those who fear Him, and delivers them.
8 Oh, taste and see that the Lord is good; blessed is the man who trusts in Him!
19 Many are the afflictions of the righteous, but the Lord delivers him out of them all. (NKJ)

Maintain Your Joy

Nehemiah 8:10

10 Then he said to them, "Go your way, eat the fat, drink the sweet, and send portions to those for whom nothing is prepared; for this day is holy to our Lord. Do not sorrow, for the joy of the Lord is your strength." (NKJ)

Trust God

Notes

Proverbs 3:5-6

5 Trust in the Lord with all your heart, and lean not on your own understanding;
6 In all your ways acknowledge Him, and He shall direct your paths. (NKJ)

Proverbs 30:5

5 Every word of God is pure; he is a shield to those who put their trust in Him. (NKJ)

DEBT REPAYMENT SCHEDULE

Debt	Total Balance	Monthly Payments	Interest Rate	Payment Past Due	Payoff Priority	Monthly Payment w/ Eliminator
Totals						

Debt to Income Ratio

Total Monthly Debt ______________

(dividcd by)

Total Monthly Gross Income__________ = ____________

(multipy by 100)

Debt/Income Ratio ____________

Debt as percentage of income	Evaluation
Less than 30%	Acceptable
31% - 35%	Fair
35% - 50%	Problematic
Greater than 50%	Debt Out of Control

© ASSET SCHEDULE - PART 1

Asset Description	Current Value	Balance Due	Net Due After Sale	Monthly Expenses	Need Index (A,B,C)	Should it be sold?
Personal Residence						
Vacation Property						
Business Real Estate						
Business Real Estate						
Business Real Estate						
Land						
Land						
Land						
Other Real Estate						
Other Real Estate						
Investments						
Investments						
Investments						
Investments						
Investments						
Retirement						
Retirement						
Retirement						

© ASSET SCHEDULE - PART 2

Asset Description	Current Value	Balance Due	Net Due After Sale	Monthly Expenses	Need Index	Should it be sold?

Eliminating Debt

Module
Study Questions

1. Debt devours resources through high interest payments.
   A) True
   B) False

2. "The borrower is servant to the lender," is found in:
   A) James 4:13
   B) Deuteronomy 28:15
   C) 1 Timothy 6:9
   D) Proverbs 22:7

3. Christians should choose bankruptcy as an option.
   A) True
   B) False

4. Which of the following scripture(s) address the importance of not becoming legally responsible for the debt or default of another?
   A) Proverbs 11:15
   B) Proverbs 22:26
   C) Proverbs 6:1-5
   D) Proverbs 17:18
   E) All of the above

5. All of the following are ways to lower your standard of living, except:
   A) Downsize house
   B) Maintain the same car
   C) Reduce eating expenses
   D) Reduce clothing expenses

6. All of the following are strategies for getting out of debt, except:
   A) Stop spending more than you currently earn
   B) Do not accumulate any more debt
   C) Establish a written budget
   D) Purchase assets that are not absolutely necessary

Module
Study Questions, continued

7. All of the following are reasons people go into debt, except:
   A) Living above your means
   B) Overuse of credit cards
   C) Not properly managing, not budgeting
   D) Financially prepared for emergencies and crises

8. Debt is considered all of the following except:
   A) It removes barriers to harmful items
   B) Slavery
   C) Presumes upon tomorrow
   D) A blessing
   E) A curse

9. "If you do not obey the voice of the Lord your God... all these curses will come upon you and overtake you," is found in:
   A) James 4:13
   B) Deuteronomy 28:15
   C) 1 Timothy 6:9
   D) Proverbs 22:7

10. Debt can also promote impulse buying and overspending.
    A) True
    B) False

11. Which of the following are assets that could potentially be sold to reduce debt?
    A) Jewelry
    B) Investments
    C) Cars
    D) Furs
    E) All of the above

12. "The wicked borrows and does not repay," is found in:
    A) 1 Peter 5:7
    B) Proverbs 3:6
    C) Psalm 37:21
    D) Luke 16:10

Workplace Wisdom Institute

13. Poor business decisions are reasons why people get into debt.
    A) True
    B) False

14. All of the following can be used to earn additional income, except:
    A) Home businesses
    B) Debt consolidation
    C) Working overtime
    D) Having teenagers work

15. Debt consolidation is usually an excellent method for reducing debt.
    A) True
    B) False

16. All of the following are strategies for getting out of debt, except:
    A) Being content with what you have
    B) Accumulating more debt
    C) Establishing a debt repayment schedule for every creditor
    D) Earning additional income

17. Surety is when a person is willing to be morally responsible for the debt or default of another.
    A) True
    B) False

18. All of the following are reasons people go into debt, except:
    A) Living below your means
    B) Acquiring status symbols
    C) Co-signing
    D) Not knowing how much you actually owe

19. Debt is money, property, or services which one person has obligated him/herself to pay another.
    A) True
    B) False

20. Debt includes all of the following except:
    A) Department store credit card or financing
    B) Money borrowed from relatives or others
    C) Home mortgages
    D) Current due bills
    E) Auto loans

Notes

Repairing
Your
Credit

Notes

Repairing Your Credit

God's Way of Doing Things

Often times we are anxious when we apply for credit because of the uncertainty of being "approved." Then, when we are approved, we are overjoyed, particularly when we receive a "credit limit" that is higher than expected. We poke out our chests to acknowledge we have received an honor.

The Value of a Good Name

Proverbs 22:1 says, *A good name is rather to be chosen than great riches* (NKJ). According to Webster's *New World College Dictionary,* credit is defined as the favorable estimate of a person's character, reputation, or good name. In the world of finance, credit runs the range of being either excellent to terrible. Evaluations and measures of credit are determined by credit bureaus—namely, Experian (formally TRW), TransUnion, Equifax, and Chilton's.

A credit bureau is an agency that serves as a clearinghouse for information on the credit rating of individuals and companies. This section deals with matters pertaining to individuals. An excellent credit rating demonstrates the individual's ability to handle payment arrangements, which have been entered into honorably. Credit agreements are contracts or covenants entered into with a lender. For a Christian, this is a very important distinction because God looks upon the relationship between creditor and lender as a vow on the part of the borrower to repay the lender the debt obligation, as agreed. The Bible tells us in:

Proverbs 22:7b

7b...the borrower is servant to the lender.

Repairing Your Credit

Numbers 30:2

2 If a man vow a vow unto the LORD, or swear an oath to bind his soul with a bond; he shall not break his word, he shall do according to all that proceedeth out of his mouth. (NKJ)

Notes

Credit is a Way of Life

It is hard to believe that prior to 1950 there were few credit cards (primarily store cards) and that people functioned financially using cash or simply saved money. Yes, they waited to purchase something until they could afford it and took pride in its ownership. However, with the advent of a non-cash society and cashless transactions, credit cards have increasingly grown to be a normal and convenient way of doing business. The new millennium presents even higher technological means of evaluating credit and cash positions with such tools as Smart cards and the like.

Today, in the Investigation Age, many corporate decisions incorporate credit history. For example, insurance policy decisions, and employment decisions consider the credit history. Banks will turn down potential candidates and insurance agencies will decline policy underwriting for poor credit.

Credit is a Double-Edge Sword

If you manage credit properly and have an excellent report, then credit is your servant. However, if you are "in financial debtor's prison," you are a slave. A serious part of this servitude is much like that of an indentured servant. An indentured servant is one who, according to Webster, enters into a contract binding to work for another for a given length of time, typically seven years. The parallel here is that your negative credit report card mark remains with the bureau for seven years or longer. In the case of filing bankruptcy, it remains for 10 years.

Notes

Repairing Your Credit, continued

Am I an Indentured Servant?

As a rule, your monthly debt obligations should not exceed 30% of your gross monthly income. If you owe more than that, you are flirting with disaster. If you answer yes to one or more the following questions on the checklist, you may be a problem debtor or reaching the point of credit danger.

1. Do you only have enough money to pay the minimum amount on your credit card statement each month?
2. Are any of your installment loans past due? Are you often late?
3. Are your charge cards borrowed to the limit?
4. Do you take cash advances on your credit cards to pay your bills?
5. Are you unable to pay real estate taxes, insurance bills, or other infrequent expenses from your current income?
6. Do you "rotate" payments to creditors, paying one this month but not the next month?
7. Do you rely on overtime or a second job to be able to pay bills?
8. Have you ever had a charge refused because your account had been suspended or because there was insufficient credit available?
9. If you lost your job, would you have an immediate financial problem?
10. Do you know how much you owe?

11. Do you get new loans to pay old ones?
12. Do you receive bills you can't remember creating?

Notes

How to Get Out of Debtor's Prison

First and foremost, recognize that according to:

2 Timothy 1:7

7 God has not given us a spirit of fear, but of power, and of love and of sound mind. (NKJ)

Your financial condition is not a surprise to God. So get over it and get busy! Fear will stop you in your tracks and forever keep you in bondage. So, bind that spirit!

Second, the resurrection power of God is living on the inside of you, by the Holy Spirit. Acts 1:8 tells us that we are endued with power:

Acts 1:8

8 you shall receive power when the Holy Spirit has come upon you. (NKJ)

So take that God-given Power, and go to work on your credit.

Lastly, you have been given a sound mind, so act like it. Do not, I say, do not get into self-condemnation, for this will paralyze you, and the devil will rule and reign in your thought life. Bring:

2 Corinthians 10:5

5 "every thought into captivity to the obedience of Christ" (KJV)

- into the obedience of the Anointing!

Notes

How to Get Out of Debtor's Prison,
continued

Practically speaking, your first defense is knowledge. God says:

Hosea 4:6

6 My people are destroyed for lack of knowledge (NKJ)

Get a copy of your credit report from each of the three major credit bureaus. Often times, there is different information being reported. If you have been turned down you are entitled to a free report. Get it.

Onward Christian Soldier

A soldier is diligent, strategic, patient, accurate and longsuffering. These are skills you will need to repair your credit. Purpose to have and maintain a good name, for the Glory of God, as a Son of God.

Step One

Verify the facts. If there are inaccuracies, fax, e-mail or call the agency and dispute the report. Call the reporting lender or store and dispute the entry. They have the fastest access to change the report. Our preference is to gather data from the lender or store, in writing, and ask them to forward the updated, accurate information to the credit-reporting agencies with a copy to you.

Step Two

It's all true. If you owe money, I advise you to honor your commitment. This will soften the blow for reviewing agencies. It shows integrity and demonstrates that you honor your word. It also can

Notes

reduce the score on the internal rating of the bureau for that particular entry. The further behind you the seven year window gets, the less important the past is and more attention is paid to the more-immediate credit history. However, if you don't pay-off the bill, the creditor can opt to reinstate the obligation for another 7-year period.

Wisdom Point

If you still owe money, the creditor can (some do, some don't) renew the claim and begin a new seven-year window. So don't try to get away with it. The ru1es are getting more and more stringent.

Step Three

Survey the Damage. Determine how much you owe, which payment is late, and how late is it. First pray and ask the Holy Spirit to give you wisdom in dealing with the creditors. Call the creditors, and make arrangements. Keep in touch with them so that they don't label you a "credit deadbeat;" some one who never intended to pay for the goods, which, by the way, you have already enjoyed using.

Don't make misleading statements if you can't pay. You must address the issues of, a) how much you can pay, and b) when you can pay.
Answering these questions makes significant progress in the mind of the creditor. A payment structure may include the total payoff, bringing the account current, or settling the account at a discount. In the budget planning and debt elimination processes you should have identified a strategy and plan.

Notes

How to Get Out of Debtor's Prison,

continued

Step Four

The Truth will Make You Free. Set up a budget and live by it. Carefully review the debt elimination section for the strategy to get out of debt. Also, review the budgeting section for recommended strategies.

Step Five

Don't Remain the Salt that has lost its Savor.

Once you have made arrangements with your creditors, be diligent about paying the debts off and remaining in contact with the creditors. When lump sums come in, pay off debt with the Debt Eliminator strategy. Keep your word and don't get off track.

Continue to give God glory as He delivers you when you take steps in the natural to restore your good name.

Insurance

Planning

Risk Management

Insurance Planning - Risk Management

Research and planning are keys to determining insurance requirements. Essential research must be done to determine the extent to which risk exists; such risks include illness, fire, theft, disability, death, car accidents, and unemployment, to name a few. While every believer is trusting God for safety, protection, and a long satisfied life, we must exercise wisdom in our stewardship over that which the Lord has blessed us.

Proverbs 27:12 states:

Proverbs 27:12

12 A prudent man foresees evil and hides himself; the simple pass on and are punished. (NKJ)

- We have the wisdom of God.
- Tools are available for us to use wisely.
- God wants us to be responsible.

A test for the insurance need is to determine, if a loss were to occur, could you sustain it?

- If your house burned down, could you rebuild it without needing any additional money or bankrupting yourself in the process?
- If there were an untimely death of a spouse, could the other spouse live and care for the children based on the pre-determined family financial income?
- If you became disabled, how long could you last with no income coming in?
- Could you buy a new car if yours was totaled in an accident?

If the answer to these questions results in the need for cash replacement and the inability to sustain the loss, then insurance is a viable vehicle to transfer or share the risk.

The Believer's Perspective Towards Insurance

Insurance for the believer can raise some fundamental faith questions regarding trust in God or the lack thereof. Please be guided by these biblical truths:

Philippians 4:19

19 But my God shall supply all your need according to his riches in glory by Christ Jesus." (KJV)

1. Believers are to NEVER put their trust in insurance policies, but in the true and living God.
2. Believers must never put their trust in insurance vehicles to "secure" their future, but must trust God for financial increase.

2 Timothy 1:7

7 For God hath not given us the spirit of fear; but of power, and of love, and of a sound mind." (KJV)

3. Believers are not to operate in fear or try to use insurance as a way to guard against that fear. Get delivered from the fear!
4. Believers are never to put their trust in "gain" or "financial enhancements" derived from insurance. God would much prefer to bless you directly and does not desire to bless you financially based on tragedy or loss.
5. Exercise sound judgment, because insurance is costly. It is more economical when purchased competitively, and more effective when it is secured for the purpose intended. (Remember most insurance {except life} is purchased in the hope that the event will NEVER occur).

Every believer has the responsibility to provide proper stewardship over the people, assets, and businesses with which God has entrusted us.

The Believer's Perspective Towards Insurance,
continued

The Word of God tells us in:

Luke 12:48b

48b..."For unto whomsoever much is given, of him shall be much required: and to whom men have committed much, of him they will ask the more." (KJV)

Risk

Risk is ever present. However we, as believers, trust in God and walk by faith. Yet, we are compelled to make decisions about how we handle risk. Many times we ignore it and hope we never have to deal with it. This is not being a wise steward of the manifold blessings of God.

Risk is a condition in which there is the possibility of an adverse result or exposure to harm or hazard. In the insurance world, risk is a peril with exposure to loss.

Risk can be:

Personal Risk

Loss of Earning Power

- Premature death
- Dependent old age
- Sickness or disability
- Unemployment

Property Risk

Direct (theft, fire, loss)

Indirect (loss of the use of the property)

Liability Risk

Unintentional injury of other persons

Damage of other's property through negligence or carelessness

Bodily injury

Risk Arising From the Failure of Others

Failure of contractor

Failure of people paying their debts

Risk can be generally handled in one of five ways:

1. Avoided – Not dealt with
2. Retained – Self-insured, you pay for the loss
3. Transferred – Insurance, Futures Contracts, Indemnity
4. Shared – Share in financial exposure of the loss (Health Care Providers, Risk Pools, FDIC)
5. Reduced – Loss Prevention and Control (i.e. safety programs, security systems)

When you secure insurance, you are sharing and transferring risk.

Life	Transfer or Sharing	No deductible
Disability	Sharing	Deductible
Auto	Sharing	Deductible
Marine	Sharing	Deductible
Health	Sharing	Deductible
Home	Sharing	Deductible
General Liability	Sharing	Deductible
Property	Sharing	Deductible

If you choose not to insure, you have either consciously or by default, self-insured. Also, if you have under-insured, that portion which represents the gap or shortfall is essentially self-insured.

To ensure that you have adequate levels of insurance, you must research, evaluate, and plan.

Risk, continued

Research the following:

- What insurance do I presently have?
- Am I insured at a level to meet my needs?
- How much does the insurance cost?
- What is the insurance company's rating?
- What type of coverage is available?

Evaluate the following:

- Different insurance options
- Varying deductible options
- Maturity and Terms of the policy
- Ability to pay the premium

Plan the following:

- Budget the expense.
- Exercise and eat healthily.
- Adequately secure the property.
- Act with a sound mind.
- Identify beneficiaries and keep policies updated.

Life Insurance

All insurance is designed to address a risk, which we hope will never happen, except life insurance.

The Word of God states:

Hebrews 9:27

27 And as it is appointed unto men once to die, but after this the judgment. (KJV)

If Jesus tarries, every believer will die unless we are in that glorious number who will be caught to meet Him in the air!

1 Thessalonians 4:17

17 Then we which are alive and remain shall be caught up together with them in the clouds, to meet the Lord in the air: and so shall we ever be with the Lord. (KJV)

The purpose of life insurance is to provide for the principle expenses that exist upon the demise of an individual and in the future for those left behind when no other source of income is available. The expenses fall into three categories, including but not limited to the following:

I. Short-Term Needs that Require Immediate Cash

a. Final Expenses for the decendent's medical, hospital, funeral, probate, attorney fees, etc.

b. Emergency funds for the family

II. Intermediate or Possibly Longer Term Needs

a. Children's Educational Fund

b. Mortgage Balance Payoff

c. Debt Repayment

d. Annual Dependent/Home Care Expenses

e. Final Tithes

f. Final Federal and State Taxes (Income Taxes)

g. Estate Taxes

h. Business Considerations

Life Insurance, continued

III. Income Continuation - Long-Term Financial Requirements

a. Spousal Living Expenses for 20, 30, 40, years including funds for retirement income subsidy

b. Funding the budget goals and objectives for the spouse, children, parents, etc.

c. Pass money on to heirs

As a part of the evaluation of life insurance needs, it is important to identify all sources of income available for survivors. The typical sources include:

- The surviving spouse's salary (if applicable)
- Decedent's life insurance policies
- Income from decedent's employee benefits
- Business Income received (if applicable)
- Income from Inheritance
- Social Security Benefits
- Veteran's Benefits

After evaluating all of the sources, it is not unusual for a capital gap to exist (better known as a shortfall). It is this shortfall that gives rise to the need for insurance. Careful evaluation and calculation should be undertaken when identifying the need for securing insurance. It should NOT be done based on multiples of income of the primary income provider (see the Insurance Appendix).

Once the life insurance needs are identified, the question of type must be explored. There are essentially two types of life insurance: Term and Permanent. Term is purchased for pure insur-

ance protection; whereas, Permanent provides protection along with a savings/investment feature.

Term Life Insurance

Term life insurance, often referred to as renting, is purchased for a specific amount over a specific time, after which it expires. Twenty-year term is in effect for 20 years and then it expires. It can be renewed and will be re-priced based on the mortality tables of the advanced age and health of the insured at the time. Also, the policy may be eligible for conversion to a permanent life policy for a hike in the premium without having to provide evidence of insurability. Term is much less costly than permanent insurance.

The disadvantage of Term insurance is its temporary nature. If used for permanent needs, it may expire at the maturation of the policy. Upon renewal, premiums are much higher due to the older age of the applicant. Annually renewable Term goes up annually.

Permanent Insurance

Permanent insurance, on the other hand, is continuous and keeps the coverage in force until the insured dies, stops paying the premium, or cancels the policy. It can be paid up, which means that the policy can be paid for in full and remain in effect until the insured dies. There is a cash-value component, which allows the insured to save or invest. The insured can borrow against the policy. The advantage of Permanent insurance is that the paid-up policy remains in place until death, and therefore provides for the permanent needs on behalf of the insured. Also, the cash value can be used to pay premiums.

Workplace Wisdom Institute

Life Insurance, continued

Within the category of permanent life insurance, there are three types:

1. Whole Life or Ordinary Life

- Participating - generally pays a dividend
- Interest-sensitive - policy holder receives excess credits
- Indeterminate Premium - lower premium but can be adjusted up to a guaranteed level
- Permanent insurance
- Ability to borrow against the policy
- Ability to use the cash value to pay premiums

2. Universal Life

- The face amount is flexible
- The premium amount is flexible
- Cash value is tied to current interest rates

3. Variable Life

- Whole life
- Cash value and death benefit vary with the value of stocks and bonds. This benefit is tied to the underlying performance of the investment.
- The death benefit is tied to the cash value, which is subject to the stock market.

- Suitable for tax-deferred investments; however, such investments can be achieved tax-deferred outside of an insurance policy and are not subject to the expense ratios.

Life insurance is a very important vehicle to help meet the financial needs of every believer. Life insurance must be entered into after thorough prayer, research, evaluation, and planning have been done.

Health Insurance

With the astronomical cost of health care, it is very important for every person to have medical coverage. One illness and the associated medical expenses can wipe out a lifetime of savings. Health insurance must be secured.

Health Insurance Sources

- Health Maintenance Organization (HMO) providers
- Fee for Service (e.g., Blue Cross/Blue Shield)
- Preferred Provider Organizations (PPOs)
- Medicare
- Medigap
- Long-Term Care
- COBRA (Consolidated Omnibus Budget Reconciliation Act)

Disability Insurance

In addition, disability insurance should be strongly considered, as studies show that a person is more likely to become disabled during their premium working years than to die. If you're in your 30's or 40's, you have an increased chance of becoming disabled than dying.

Disability Insurance, continued

There are three key issues in researching, evaluating, and planning to purchase disability insurance:

1. How much coverage is enough, given the amount of income that you earn and given the cost of the insurance?
2. Is the definition of disability clearly understood? It is more expensive to secure insurance for disability from a specific job/ profession which you are performing. For example, an orthodontist being insured for that job will pay more than being insured to simply perform any job.
3. The waiting period ranges from 30 to 120 days, with 30-day increments (30-60-90-120). The earlier you need the benefit to kick in, the more the premium will cost.

Make an accurate assessment, because disability insurance is expensive. Also, evaluate how much disability insurance you already have: it may be available to you as a benefit of your employment.

Determine in advance, the benefit period, the renewability and non-cancelability, the cost of living escalator, and waiver of premium.

Homeowners' Insurance

It is common knowledge that a person's largest expense is the purchase of a home. As stewards of the blessings of God, we are called to protect this investment. One way to protect the investment is to provide an effective security system. Another is to share the risk and purchase homeowner's insurance.

The key to purchasing homeowner's insurance is making sure that you have enough to replace your home in the event of a loss/fire or in the event of theft. This is not the place to cut corners in the budget. Historically, policies were written with the Rule of 80, which

meant that as long as the house was insured for 80% of the replacement cost (established by the insurance company or by an appraisal), then the house would be replaced despite the cost of replacement. However, due to the financial exposure of insurance companies, many states have allowed insurance companies to change their underwriting policies. Insurance companies are now insuring up to a predetermined value. In Michigan the standard is 120%, but it can be bought up to 140%.

An example of this is as follows:

Purchase Price	$ 80,000
House Replacement Cost*	$100,000
120% Value	$120,000 maximum available for build out

*predetermined by insurance company

Formerly Rule of 80

House Replacement Cost*	$100,000
Insurance Covered:	$ 80,000
Actual Replacement Cost	$200,000 or unlimited

In the past, the insurance company would pay an uncapped value to replace the house. This is now capped at a predetermined value.

You must determine if you have the proper policy coverage, and whether the policy is appropriate and adequate. Review replacement cost value at least yearly.

You must have an inventory of everything in the house. A videotape is highly recommended. It should be kept OUTSIDE of the house. Keep receipts for items that are important, expensive, and difficult to replace. Use a safe deposit box, if necessary. (See Insurance Appendix.)

Workplace Wisdom Institute

Homeowners' Insurance, continued

Schedule all personal property such as jewelry, furs, art collections, Persian rugs, golf clubs, silverware, cameras, musical instruments, etc. through the Home Owner's Scheduled Personal Property Endorsement.

Finally, read the policy. Keep your policy current as you add to your home (i.e. remodeling, building additions, art collections, etc.) If personal cash flow is limited, consider increasing the deductible, which will lower the premium payment.

Schedules have been provided for the reader to complete an inventory of all assets and personal property. (See Insurance Appendix)

Automobile Insurance

Due to the number of automobile thefts and accidents that occur every day in the United States of America, wisdom demands that automobile insurance be secured. Further, the law requires it. Economic losses total in the billions of dollars every year in auto-related accidents.

Review your present coverage:

Type of Insurance	Current Coverage	Desirable Coverage
Liability Insurance		(000's)
Bodily Injury		$250/500
Property Damage		$250/500
Umbrella (if necessary)		$1 million
Collision		Highest Affordable
Comprehensive		Highest Affordable
Medical Coverage		$10
Un-(Under-) insured Motorist		$250/500

* Umbrella insurance is secured in excess of existing policies and requires the insured to maintain higher limits of insurance to qualify. It is very economical.

Evaluate your present insurance policies and determine whether the coverage you presently have is adequate. If you cannot meet the recommended levels, view the listed amounts as a target for the future, and begin to plan for them in your budget as you go to the wealthy place.

Workplace Wisdom Institute

Notes

Insurance Planning

Risk Management

Appendix

LIFE INSURANCE PRODUCT ANALYZER

Insuring the Present Values in Your Life

	General Description	Investment Vehicle	Investment Flexibility	Premium Flexibility	Face Amount Flexibility	Appropriate For
TERM-Mortality & Expenses ONLY						
Annual Renewable	Lowest Cost	NONE	N/A	NONE Increases Yearly	NONE	Very limited situations
Level Premium Term and Convertible Term	Quality Term After Tax Life Insurance	NONE	N/A	NONE Fixed for Life of Policy	NONE	Limited Cash Flow Temporary Needs Protection NOW
TERM "PLUS"-Mortality & Expenses "PLUS" ADDITIONAL DOLLARS FOR INVESTMENT						
Whole Life	Tried and True Basic Coverage Dividends paid	Insurance Co. selected Long-term bonds and mortgages	NONE To change investment of capital, borrowing from the policy and reinvesting is required.	NONE Billed premium remains level. Dividends can provide reduction or elimination. Loans Available.	NONE If you want more, you buy new, IF you can pass a physical.	The Conservative Older Insureds Substandard Insureds

Life Insurance for Protection and Profit

Universal Life	*"How much would you like to pay... When?"*	*Annual Interest Sensitive Investments*	**NONE** *To charge investment of capital requires WITHDRAWAL of capital.*	**MAXIMUM** *Just enough for Mortality and expenses, of AS MUCH AS LAW ALLOWS.*	*Increase it or decrease it as it suits your life situation...Stay Healthy for major increases.*	*Younger Insureds Variable Needs Like short-term interest rate investments.*
Variable Life	*We will put it where You want it.*	*Common Stock Bond Funds Guaranteed Interest Rates Zero Coupons Money Markets etc., etc....*	*You Name it. You Split it. You Move it. You Borrow it. Both fixed and variable rates.*	**NONE** *Billed premium remains level. Loans Available.*	**NONE** *If you want more, you buy new, IF you can pass a physical.*	*The Investor. An alternative to ....Buy Term, Invest Difference.*
Universal Variable Life	*"You Decide!" How much.... Where.....When?*	*Common Stock Bond Funds Guaranteed Interest Rates Zero Coupons Money Markets etc., etc....*	*You Name It. You Split It. You Move It. You Withdraw It.*	**MAXIMUM** *Just enough for Mortality and expenses, of AS MUCH AS LAW ALLOWS.*	*Increase it or decrease it as it suits your life situation...Stay Healthy for major increases.*	*The Investor. An alternative to ....Buy Term, Invest Difference. I want it MY WAY!*

Notes:

Source: Adapted from Practicing Financial Planning, a Complete Guide for Professionals by Sid Mittra, 1993.

What are your life insurance needs?

SUMMARY STATEMENT

Obligations

Homeowner (outstanding mortgage loan balance and real estate taxes) or Renter (Annual rent x years)	$________
Credit Card Debt	$________
Outstanding Loans	$________
Children's Education Fund	$________
Emergency Cash Fund (cash needed immediately)	$________
Family Living Expenses (money needed to continue present lifestyle)	$________
Child Care Fund (money needed to keep children under paid supervision)	$________
Retirement Fund	$________
Other (final expenses, estate taxes)	$________
Total Obligations	$________

Personal Funds

Savings	$________
Checking	$________
Stocks, Bonds, Mutual Funds	$________
Other Investments (pension, profit sharing, property)	$________
Group Life Insurance	$________
Personal Life Insurance	$________
Other (Social Security)	$________
Total Personal Funds	$________

Total Obligations	$________
Total Personal Funds (Less)-	$________
Total Life Insurance Needed	$________

STEP ONE: *What would your family's needs be if you were to die today?*

A. Final Expenses

- Final medical and Hospital costs
- Funeral
- Attorney/executor fees
- Probate costs

Total Needed $ ________________

(Estimate 85% of your annual income for "Total Needed." Individuals with large estates should consult with an Estate Tax Specialist regarding estate taxes.)

B. Emergency Fund

- Major home repairs
- Auto repairs
- Medical emergencies

Total Needed $ ________________

(Estimate 85% of your annual income for "Total Needed")

C. Children's Education Fund

______________	X	______________	= $	____________
Total cost of degree		*Number of Children*		*Total Needed*

(As an estimate, the average annual cost of tuition for a 4-year, in-state public university is approximately $3,000 and $17,000 for a private university. Current average room and board costs are $10,000 per year. Books and other fees should be included as well.)

D. Mortgage Balance

$ ________________

E. Debt Repayment

- Auto loans ____________
- Home equity loan ____________
- Credit card balances ____________
- Other ____________

Total Needed $____________

F. Annual Dependent/Home Care Expenses

- Care for dependent ____________
- Home maintenance ____________
- Food/Clothing ____________

Total Needed **$**____________

(Estimate 85% of your annual income for "*Annual Amount* ")

____________ X ____________ = $____________

Annual Amount — *Number of years to continue support* — *Total Needed*

Grand total needed from
Sections A-F

$____________

STEP TWO: *What are your existing liquid assets, life insurance policies*?

- Life insurance *(including group life policy)* ____________
- Cash and savings accounts ____________
- Other liquid assets ____________

Total available liquid
Assets and insurance **$**____________

STEP THREE: *Calculate the amount of additional life insurance you need*

Total cash needed from STEP ONE: (sections A-F)		$ ________
Minus total available liquid *Assets and existing life* *Insurance from STEP TWO*	_	$ ________
Additional life Insurance needed	=	$ ________

In order to protest your family's financial security, how much can you comfortably set aside each month to meet this need?
$

Evaluate your life insurance needs and review this assessment with an insurance professional.

Home Inventory for Insurance Accountability Purposes

JEWELRY	No.	Repl. Cost	Present Value
Watches			
Rings			
Necklaces			
Pendants			
Bracelets			
Earrings			
Pins, brooches			
TOTAL			

FURS	No.	Repl. Cost	Present Value
Coats			
Capes			
Jackets			
Stoles			
Scarfs			
TOTAL			

FINE ARTS	No.	Repl. Cost	Present Value
Paintings			
Etchings			
Statuary			
Figurines			
TOTAL			

SILVER		Repl. Cost	Present Value
Place settings			
Serving pieces			
Platters, trays			
Dishes, bowls			
Chafing dishes			
Tea service			
Pitchers			
Candle holders			
Other pieces			
TOTAL			

CHINA, LINENS	No.	Repl. Cost	Present Value
China dinnerware			
Luncheon sets			
Breakfast sets			
Table cloths			
Napkins			
Place mats			
TOTAL			

CRYSTAL	No.	Repl. Cost	Present Value
Goblets			
Glasses, tumblers			
Sherbet, parfait			
Punch bowl sets			
Cocktail glasses			
Bowls, vases			
Pitchers			
Decanters			
Dishes			
TOTAL			

RECREATION		Repl. Cost	Present Value
Pianos			
Organs			
Musical instruments			
Television sets			
Surround Sound System			
CDs			
Radios			
Tape recorders			
Videos			
Big Screen TVs			
TOTAL			

Home Inventory for Insurance Accountability Purposes

BEDROOMS	1			2			3		
Articles	**No.**	**Repl. Cost**	**Present Value**	**No.**	**Repl. Cost**	**Present Value**	**No.**	**Repl. Cost**	**Present Value**
Carpets									
Draperies									
Curtains									
Beds/springs									
Mattresses									
Dressers									
Chests									
Vanities									
Chaise Lounges									
Chairs									
Benches									
Tables									
Night Stands									
Desks									
Secretaries									
Lamps									
Pictures									
Wall Hangings									
Mirrors									
Vanity Appt's									
Décor									
Baby Cribs									
Playpens									
Bassinettes									
Nursery Access.									
TOTAL									

Notes:

Home Inventory for Insurance Accountability Purposes

LIVING AREAS					DINING AREAS	
Articles	**No.**	**Replacement Costs**	**Present Value**	**No.**	**Replacement Cost**	**Present Value**
Carpets						
Draperies						
Curtains						
Sofas						
Studio Couches						
Lounge Chairs						
Occas. Chairs						
Straight Chairs						
Slip Covers						
Pillows						
Tables						
Table Access.						
Desks						
Secretaries						
Desk Access.						
Room Dividers						
Planters						
Lamps						
Pictures						
Wall Hangings						
Mirrors						
Clocks						
Décor						
Fireside Fixtures						
TV Tables						
TOTAL						

Notes:

Home Inventory for Insurance Accountability Purposes

PERSONAL EFFECTS		Husband		PERSONAL EFFECTS		Wife	
Articles	**No.**	**Repl. Cost**	**Present Value**		**No.**	**Repl. Cost**	**Present Value**
Suits				Day dresses			
Formal attire				Party dresses			
Sports coats				Formals			
Sports jackets				Suits			
Slacks				Coats			
Overcoats				Jackets			
Topcoats				Sweaters			
Sweaters				Skirts			
Sportswear				Blouses			
Beach wear				Slacks, jeans			
Shorts				Bermuda shorts			
Hats, caps				Beach wear			
Gloves				Sportswear			
Shoes, Loafers				Hats, gloves			
Slippers				Purses, billfolds			
Boots				Shoes, slippers			
Belts				Galoshes, boots			
Shirts				Belts			
Ties				Hosiery, scarves			
Socks				Handkerchiefs			
Under shorts				Lingerie			
Handkerchiefs				Robes			
Pajamas				Housecoats			
Robes				Sleep wear			
Billfolds				Umbrellas			
Men's jewelry				Luggage			
Luggage				Costume jewelry			
Electric razors				Cosmetics			
				Hair dryers			
TOTAL				**TOTAL**			

Notes:

Home Inventory for Insurance Accountability Purposes

PERSONAL EFFECTS	Male Child			PERSONAL EFFECTS	Female Child		
Articles	**No.**	**Repl. Cost**	**Present Value**		**No.**	**Repl. Cost**	**Present Value**
School apparel				School dresses			
Suits				Church dresses			
Slacks				Playwear			
Shirts				Coats			
Sports jackets				Jackets			
Sportswear				Sweaters			
Sweaters				Skirts			
Dress coat				Blouses			
Beach wear				Slacks, jeans			
Shorts				Shorts			
Hats, caps				T-Shirts			
Gloves				Beach wear			
Shoes, Loafers				Hats, gloves			
Slippers				Purses, billfolds			
Boots				Shoes, slippers			
Belts				Galoshes, boots			
Shirts				Belts			
Ties				Hosiery, scarves			
Socks				Handkerchiefs			
Under shorts				Pajamas			
Handkerchiefs				Robes			
Pajamas				Housecoats			
Robes				Umbrellas			
Billfolds				Luggage			
Luggage				Costume Jewelry			
				Hair dryers			
TOTAL				**TOTAL**			

Notes:

Home Inventory for Insurance Accountability Purposes

Kitchen				Appliances			
Item	**No.**	**Repl. Cost**	**Present Value**	**Item**	**No.**	**Repl. Cost**	**Present Value**
Stoves				Rotisseries			
Refrigerator				Roasters			
Freezer				Coffee maker			
Dishwasher				Mixer, blender			
Cookware				Toasters			
Cutlery				Waffle irons			
Utensils				Grill, griddle			
Food				Fry pans			
Clocks				Knives			
Décor				Sharpeners			
				Can openers			
				Electric toothbrushes			
TOTAL				**TOTAL**			

Yard				Utility			
Item	**No.**	**Repl. Cost**	**Present Value**	**Item**	**No.**	**Repl. Cost**	**Present Value**
Outdoor furniture				Washer			
Pool accessories				Dryer			
Cooking equipment				Iron			
Power mowers				Ironing board			
Lawn sweepers				Sewing machine			
Snow plows				Vacuum cleaner			
Tillers				Floor polisher			
Edger				Shampooer			
Trimmers				Cleaning supplies			
Garden hose							
Sprinkler							
Spreader							
Garden equipment							
TOTAL				**TOTAL**			

Notes:

Home Inventory for Insurance Accountability Purposes

Bedding				Appliances			
Item	**No.**	**Repl. Cost**	**Present Value**	**Item**	**No.**	**Repl. Cost**	**Present Value**
Blankets				Rotisseries			
Quilts				Roasters			
Pillows				Coffee maker			
Sheets				Mixer, blender			
Electric				Toasters			
Cutlery				Waffle irons			
Utensils				Grill, griddle			
Food				Fry pans			
Clocks				Knives			
Décor				Sharpeners			
TOTAL				Can openers			
Bathroom				Electric toothbrushes			
Bath towels				Mattress covers			
Hand towels				**TOTAL**			
Wash clothes				Miscellaneous			
Bath accessories				Air Conditioner			
Bath mats				Fans, heaters			
Scale				Dehumidifiers			
Bath rugs				Computers			
Drapes				Calculators			
Shower curtains				Files			
TOTAL				**TOTAL**			
Leisure				Leisure			
Golf clubs				Games			
Fishing gear				Toys			
Firearms				Playground			
Bowling				Art supplies			
Tennis				Coin collection			
Ice skates				Stamp collection			
Camping				Camera equipment			
Ski equipment				Camcorder			
Bicycles				Power tools			
Billiard				Hand tools			
Card table				Other equip			
Card chairs				Books			
TOTAL				**TOTAL**			

Notes:

Home Inventory for Insurance Accountability Purposes

Summary of Inventory			
Description	No. of Items	Replacement Cost	Present Value
Living Areas			
1.			
2.			
3.			
Dining Areas			
1.			
2.			
Bedroom(s)			
1.			
2.			
3.			
4.			
Personal Effects			
Husband			
Wife			
Male child			
Female child			
Jewelry			
China, Linens			
Crystal			
Furs			
Fine art			
Silver			
Kitchen			
Utility			
Appliances			
Yard			
Bedding			
Bathroom			
Leisure			
Insurance type(s)			
Homeowners			
Valuables			
Automobile			
Health			
Life			
TOTAL			

Notes:

Home Inventory for Insurance Accountability Purposes

Insurance			
Type of Insurance	**Cash Value**		**Amount/Limit of Insurance**
Homeowners Insurance /_/ Basic Form /_/ Broad Form /_/ "All Risks" Form			
Dwelling			
Detached Structure			
Additional Living Expense			
Personal Property on Premises			
Personal Property away from Premises			
Family / Personal Liability			
TOTAL			
"All Risks" for Valuables			
Yacht / Motor Boat(s)			
Liability			
TOTAL			
Automobile Insurance	**Car #1**	**Car #2**	
Bodily Injury			
Property Damage			
Medical			
Collision			
Comprehensive			
TOTAL			
Health Insurance	**Type**	**Amount**	
Disability Income			
Major Medical			
Hospitalization			
Other			
TOTAL			
Life Insurance	**Type**	**Amount**	
TOTAL			

Notes:

Home Inventory for Insurance Accountability Purposes

Summary of Insurance				
Total Premium	Term	Annual Cost	Renewal Premium Due	Company or Agency

Notes:

Investment

Planning

When Jesus talked about money, it was primarily in the context of paying off debts, saving, or investing.

Honoring The Debt Obligation

Jesus paid his debts and the debts of others. In Matthew 17:24 and 27, after Jesus and his disciples arrived in Capernaum, the collectors of the two-drachma tax came to Peter and asked, "Doesn't your teacher pay the temple tax?" Jesus replied. "But so that we may not offend them, go to the lake and throw out your line. Take the first fish you catch; open its mouth and you will find a four-drachma coin. Take it and give it to them for my tax and yours." (NIV)

Jesus Admonishes For Not Investing

Jesus said in Luke 19:22,23 "His master replied, 'I will judge you by your own words, you wicked servant! You knew, did you, that I am a hard man, taking out what I did not put in, and reaping what I did not sow? Why then didn't you put my money on deposit, so that when I came back, I could have collected it with interest?'" (NIV)

Jesus said, "Thou oughtest therefore to have *put my money to the exchangers,* and then at my coming I should have received mine own with usury." Matthew 25:7, in the Parable of the Talents - Investments.

Jesus Rewards Those Who Have Invested Wisely

Matthew 25:19-21,"After a long time the master of those servants returned and settled accounts with them. The man who had received the five talents brought the other five. 'Master,' he said, 'you entrusted me with five talents. See, I have gained five more.' "His master replied, 'Well done, good and faithful servant! You have been faithful with a few things; I will put you in charge of many things. Come and share your master's happiness!'" (NIV)

If you are not getting a return on the money that God has entrusted you with, you need to increase your level of stewardship.

Investment Planning

In order to invest and get a return, you must have a financial plan that is broad and inclusive of investments. Jesus is saying to, minimally, have a savings account generating at least a modest return on your investments.

The first goal of investing is to have a 6-month Emergency Fund set aside, a savings or money market account, to meet any unexpected financial obligations. Many financial advisors may recommend 3 months, however, we have found that a six-month supply of liquidity (cash or cash equivalents) is adequate to meet the needs of a family if the situation becomes prolonged. In exercising wisdom, it is better to have more than enough than not enough.

In developing a Financial Plan for investing, you should consider the following:

A. Where am I financially today?

B. What are my financial goals for the next 5 to 15 years?

C. How do I plan to meet my short, intermediate, and long term goals?

D. What major expenses must I plan for?

For example, marriage, children, new home, education, "retirement," dream vacation, starting a business, leaving an inheritance for my children and grandchildren, leaving an endowment to my church (a large sum of money for perpetuity), helping aging parents.

For the believer, it is important that we realize and act on the fact that God has called us to do things decently and in order (1Corinthians 14:40, "Let all things be done decently and in order"). (KJV) Therefore, we should be preparing for events that are important to us, not at the last minute, but well in advance.

Workplace Wisdom Institute

Jesus Rewards Those Who Have Invested Wisely,

continued

Some readers may say, "But time has already gone by and it's late in the financial game for me." Well, bless God, He can redeem the time if you become diligent and faithful to put a financial plan in place, live by it, and work the plan!

Investment Planning is associated with everything we do because it determines whether we have a vision of accumulating wealth and preserving it. Investment planning, by design, must be undertaken in stages; namely, short term, which is a year; intermediate term or 3-5 years; and long term, which is 7-10 years or more. In order for investment planning to be successful, the investor must play the central role in achieving the delicate balance between risk and reward.

The classic risk-return relationship is illustrated below. On the X Axis is the rate of return, and the Y-Axis represents the risk level. The plane represents the degree of risk assumed in relationship to the reward of return. A person should not be investing large sums of money prior to having a six (6) month emergency fund saved.

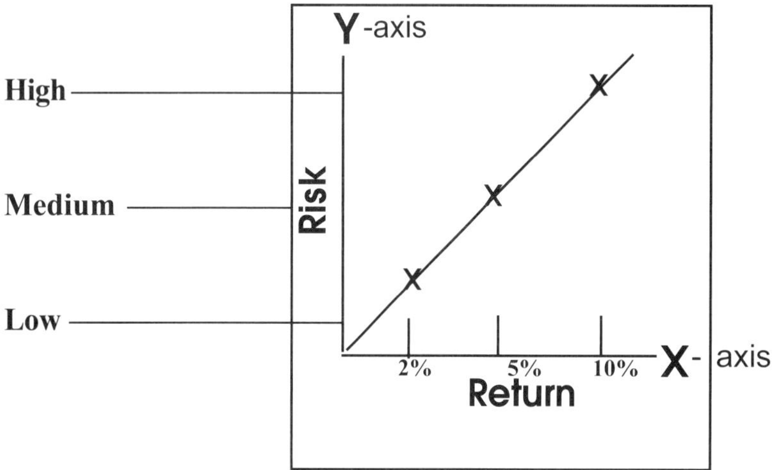

The greater the risk, the higher the return

What generally happens to many new, and even seasoned, investors is that the attraction of high return on investments or up-side down-plays the reality of their ability to absorb the risk.

It is imperative that each investor determine their risk-aversion level in relationship to the investment *prior* to investing. This requires due diligence, or research. The investor must know their personal goals, objectives, risk-aversion levels, the expected returns on investment, the time horizons, and the tax implications. (See the Investment Appendix - Asset Allocation Portfolio)

In order to plan effectively, the investor must consider the following:

The Law of Compounding Interest

The reason why Jesus told the investors that they were good and faithful was because He knew that time was on the side of the investor. Money invested will grow over time. Sure, losses may occur, but over time they can be regained. An investment cycle is generally 7 years. The older a person gets, the fewer investment cycles are available in their lifetime. Depending on the purpose of investment, the funds may be needed to support children's educational costs, "retirement lifestyle," or other financial obligations, including gifting to the church, which is sooner than planned.

The younger a person is when they begin investing, the greater the opportunity for investment growth and, thereby, wealth accumulation. The principle, which is at play, there is called "The Law of Compounding Interest." It simply states that if you invest $100.00 today at 4% per annum, at the end of the year the hundred dollars will have earned $4. Most importantly, at the beginning of year two, the principle balance of $104.00 is now earning interest at the rate of 4%. At the end of year two, the principle of $104.00 will have earned $8.16. Interest has been earned on interest, and the effect is a multiplier. This is known as having your money work for you or having your money earn money while you are doing something else.

Workplace Wisdom Institute

A further example of the impact of "The Law of Compounding Interest" is demonstrated as follows:

Principle Investment	Interest Rate/ Return	**Year One** Cumulative Growth	**Year Five** Cumulative Growth	**Year Ten** Cumulative Growth	**Year Twenty** Cumulative Growth
A) $1,000	1.5%	$1,015.00	$1,077.28	$1,160.54	$1,346.86
B) $1,000	4%	$1,040.00	$1,216.65	$1,480.24	$2,191.12
C) $1,000	5%	$1,050.00	$1,276.28	$1,628.89	$2,653.30
D) $1,000	7.5%	$1,075.00	$1,435.63	$2,061.03	$4,247.85
E) $1,000	9%	$1,090.00	$1,538.62	$2,367.36	$5,605.41
F) $1,000	10%	$1,100.00	$1,610.51	$2,593.74	$6,727.50
G) $1,000	12%	$1,120.00	$1,762.34	$3,105.85	$9,646.29

One can clearly see that time has worked to the advantage of the investor. Conversely, if the investor has a short-time horizon, the return will be significantly less assuming all conditions remain the same as stated above.

Therefore, the investor is strongly advised to begin investing immediately upon securing 6 months of emergency funds. There are various life cycle stages of investing that are dependent on the age and circumstances of the investor.

Life Cycle Stages

Investment goals change as a person matures. Generally, there are three stages:

A) Accumulation – this stage generally includes:

- Protecting one's family
- Providing for children's education
- Accumulating basic assets, homes, furnishings
- Building cash reserves and emergency funds

At this stage of growth, a portfolio generally consists of a large percentage of cash reserves and a variety of low risk investments to help the investor's savings grow at a slow but steady rate.

B) Acceleration – This stage generally includes:

- Peak earning years
- Increase in risk taking
- Focus on growth
- Maximizing net worth
- Higher rate of return expectations

At this point, the investor is ready to grow exponentially. The investor can be much more aggressive because they have time to recoup losses, have studied and researched their investment strategy, have accumulated their cash reserves, made major purchases, and can now grow their net worth.

C) Preservation – This stage includes:

- Sunset of the peak earning years
- Inability to bounce back as in earlier years
- Lower risk aversion level due to age
- Potential need for capital to meet health and living requirements

Life Cycle Stages, (continued)

Capital preservation is the strategy of concern at this point for the "retirement type" life style. At this stage in life, it is God's best that every believer operate in glory days, not trying to rob Peter to pay Paul.

The above stages are provided to introduce to some and remind others of the traditional life cycles of investing. We have observed some interesting behavior on the part of senior citizens in the decade of the 1990s. Due to low returns in the liquidity markets, the elderly began to invest in the stock market, flooding it with hundreds of millions of dollars. However, when the market began to downturn during the turn of the century, we began to witness portfolios diminishing and seniors losing money once set aside for retirement.

Careful planning is a requirement and should not be done based on fear or greed.

Investment Risks

There are five fundamental investment systematic risks, which are non-diversifiable. This means that the risk affects all returns on all comparable investments; therefore, these risks are across the board:

- **Interest Rate Risk**

  Uncertainty associated with fluctuations in the interest rate which could potentially result in loss on investment

- **Market Risk**

  Potential that the market as a whole may decline

Workplace Wisdom Institute

- **Reinvestment Rate Risk**

  Potential that the investor may not earn as much through reinvestment as was anticipated when the investment was initially made

- **Purchasing Power Risk**

  Potential that inflation will erode the value of the currency

- **Exchange Rate Risk**

  Conversion of currency risk

There are two additional risks, which are unsystematic; that is, that they are diversifiable. They have to do with individual or company events that affect the securities. An example may be the laying off of 7,000 employees, a recall which affects the company's profitability and in turn results in the company not paying a dividend to the stockholders. The specific risks are:

- **Business Risk**

  The level of risk associated with the specific type of business (i.e., the restaurant business, speculative businesses, e-businesses).

- **Financial Risk**

  The level of risk associated with the sources of financing, how leveraged the company is and, in a down turn, whether it will face ruin or bankruptcy due to lack of inability to service its debt.

When considering investing, the educated investor must consider each of these risks in relationship to its return and in relationship to the investor's appetite for risk.

Investment Risks, (continued)

Diversification

An investor's portfolio should be diversified. Exposure in one sector or one stock, all bonds, or all cash typically works against the investor and provides extraordinary risk unnecessarily. Such risk-taking has been known to happen. For example, in 2001, the Enron Corporation filed U. S. Chapter 11 Bankruptcy, and the stock hit rock bottom, resulting in many employee stockholders who were not diversified losing all their retirement savings.

Diversification helps control risk. Rarely can an investor select the right investments, at the right time, and liquidate them at the right time. However, based upon one's life cycle, return requirements, and risk-aversion level, a diversified portfolio can be structured to address investment objectives and reduce risk. Diversification is achieved by reducing risk within a particular asset class by spreading individual issues of stocks, bonds, or other investments within a broad range.

Asset Allocation

Market timing is virtually impossible. In fact, more than 94% of the total return on your investment dollars is a result of the way you allocate your resources. Only 6% depends on the specific assets you buy. (Ernst and Young Personal Financial Planning Guide 3rd Ed., 1999). Asset Allocation maximum return and minimum risk scenarios and recommendations are located in the Appendix.

Asset Allocation is using different investment vehicles – cash, bonds, stock, real estate, and so on – to accomplish investment objectives. The basic components are a statistical evaluation of investment risk measured in relationship to the expected return, which drives diversification to achieve the expected return at the least possible rate of risk.

Investment Vehicles

There are basically six categories or classes.

Investment Planning

The three primary investment categories are:

- Cash and Cash Equivalents
- Bonds, also called Fixed Income Securities
- Stocks, also called Equities

In addition there are:

- Real Estate
- Natural Resources, including oil and gas
- Tangibles, such as gold and silver

For the believer, there is a seventh category, which is "the God-given idea," which God has given you. This investment is guaranteed to return 100-fold and is your best opportunity to ***Dominate Money*** and go to the wealthy place.

Cash and Cash Equivalents comprise:

- Savings and Checking Accounts
- Money Market Deposit Accounts
- U.S. Government Series EE bonds
- Certificates of Deposit (CDs)
- Money Market Mutual Funds
- U.S. Treasury Bills
- Guaranteed Investment Contracts (GICs)
- Commercial Paper

Bonds or Fixed-Income Securities

There is a very wide range of bond issues and issuers, ranging from U. S. Government Bonds, which are the most secure, to High-Yield Corporate Junk Bonds. Bonds are debt obligations of the issuer. The purchase of a bond transfers cash in the form of a loan to the issuer, in exchange for a yield or interest

Bonds or Fixed Income Securities, (continued)

payment to the bondholder. The issuer must pay interest at a fixed rate, known as the coupon rate, which is dictated by a set schedule, usually semi-annually.

Also, the issuer must pay the face value of the bond when it matures–which can be anywhere from one to thirty years from the date of issue. Bonds that come due in ten or fewer years are frequently called notes. In general, you may cash in a bond at any time and do not have to hold it to maturity.

A bond that does not pay out over its life is the zero coupon bond, which is purchased at a discount on the face value and pays out at a premium at maturity.

Bonds are generally considered stable, safe, and dependable. Bonds are fixed-income investments; which means the payments you receive will stay the same over the life of the bond or, in other words, (until it matures).

While fixed-income securities tend to be stable, they are subject to interest rate, and inflation rate fluctuations, and default risks. The longer the maturity of the bond, the greater the risk; therefore, the bond holder should expect to receive a higher rate of return.

Interest Rate Risk

Bonds usually operate in an inverse relationship to the interest rate. When the interest rate is low, theoretically, the bond rate is high. Conversely, when interest rates are high, bond rates are low. If a bondholder keeps the bond until maturity, there is no fluctuation. However, if the bondholder sells the security prior to maturity, depending on the current market condition, it could affect the price of the bond.

For example, you buy a bond at par which is $1,000 for a yield of 8% (or a current yield of $80 per year). A year later rates are down, making the price of your bond more attractive. A new investor could buy your bond for $1,100. If you were to sell your bond in

such a market environment, you would realize capital appreciation in the value of the bond price. The purchaser, on the other hand, would realize a change in the current yield. The rate remains the same, at 8%, but the current yield changes from 8% to approximately 7.3% ($80 divided by the new price of the bond, $1,100).

Generally, the yield curve from short-term treasuries to 30-year treasury bonds increases, meaning as the date at which the bond comes due increases, the yield or interest rate paid is higher. Increased risk, increased reward. However, there are periods when there is what is known as an inverted yield curve, which signals possible recession or lower rates. The result is that the long-term yields do not support the maturity because the yield is not worth the length of the term of the bond.

Default Risk

Bonds are rated by what is known as *rating agencies.* The most noteworthy agencies are Moody's, and Standard and Poor's. These two agencies evaluate and rate the ability of the company or issuer to repay the bond holder and make the coupon or interest payments. The risk here is that the company or the issuer will default and fail to pay its debt obligations, possibly going out of business, filing bankruptcy, or experiencing extreme cash flow deficits disabling the company from paying the coupon rate.

Inflation Rate Risk

Inflation is always the enemy of investments, because of its ability to depreciate the future value of money. The risk refers to the loss of value in your investments caused by the depreciation of the currency. If inflation is constant, this does not pose as much of a risk as a rises in the inflation rate. For example, if you buy a long-term bond when inflation is low, such as the present market environment (inflation rate 2.5%), and inflation increases, both your bond resale value and the value of the interest you receive will decline.

Bonds

The most widely traded types of bonds include the following:

U. S. Government Securities

Treasury Notes

Treasury Bonds

Inflation Indexed Securities

Zero-Coupon Treasury Securities

Agency Bonds

Municipal Securities

State and Local Government Bonds

- Tax Anticipation Notes
- General Obligation Bonds
- Revenue Bonds

Corporate Bonds

Secured and Unsecured Bonds

Debentures

Characteristics

- May be callable
- Floating Rate Bonds
- Convertible Bonds
- Spread may be 75 to 100 basis points higher than Treasuries

Mortgage Backed Securities

Issued by Federal agencies, which purchase mortgages from Banks

- GNMA "Ginnie Mae"
- FHLMC "Freddie Mac"
- FNMA "Fannie Mae"
- CMOs - Collateralized Mortgage Obligations
- REMICs - Real Estate Mortgage Investment Conduits

Characteristics

- Default risk is minimal
- Prepayment Risk can be substantial
- Large principal repayment – low return

Junk bonds are high-yield and high-risk corporate issues with low-grade rating.

The background of the bonds issuer must be researched. The role of bonds in a portfolio is key to diversification in the asset class of fixed-income investments. However, risk must be evaluated in relationship to the investor's level of tolerance.

Stocks

Stocks represent ownership in a company. The stockholder owns a "piece of the action" and as a result takes a risk. If the company is profitable and generates earnings after all obligations are paid, a dividend is declared and payments are issued to the stockholders.

There are different types of companies that are at different levels of capitalization. The level of capitalization determines the market capitalization class within which it falls:

Stocks, continued

- Large Capitalization Stocks – Market capitalization of more than $5 billion
- Mid-Capitalization Stocks – Market capitalization between $1 - $5 Billion
- Small Capitalization Stocks – Market capitalization of less than $1 Billion

Market capitalization is defined by the per-share price of a company multiplied by the number of outstanding shares.

Stocks are generally categorized as follows:

- Income Stocks

  Steady in the form of dividend income
- Growth – Income Stocks

  Respectable dividend and Growth
- Growth Stocks

  Fast-growing companies, usually no dividend

  Possible loss of principal

  High risk
- Aggressive Growth

  Young fast-growing companies

  Reinvest earnings, if any

  Share price is volatile

  You could lose all principal

Workplace Wisdom Institute

- Value Stocks

    Stock is undervalued

    Presumed - Good buy

- Cyclical Stocks

    Earnings tend to follow a business cycle (i.e., retail, auto, etc.)

- Defensive Stocks

    Stable even during economic volatility (i.e., utilities)

- Blue Chip Stocks

    Top proven performers in the market. Usually, good in up and down markets. Dividends consistently paid out.

How to Purchase a Stock

Research and more research! You must perform a fundamental analysis, which includes:

a) Research the Company

   i. Profitability

   ii. Management

   iii. Return of Equity

b) Research the Stock

   i. Historical Trading Range

   ii. Earnings Per Share

   iii. Price/Earnings Ratio

Stocks, continued

iv. Book Value per Share

v. Dividend History

c) Industry Analysis

i. Determine the characteristics

ii. Evaluate the stage of growth of the company within the industry

iii. Determine whether the industry is stable or volatile

A thorough analysis should be completed on a stock prior to purchasing it. You need to learn as much as possible about the stock market and the particular stock well in advance of investing. A stock tip given to you by someone based on a hunch often results in unmet expectations.

If you do not have time to complete all the research on your own, you can retain a broker or advisor. There are varying levels of brokers and brokerage houses; the fees associated with them vary as well.

They include:

- Full Service Brokers
- Independent Investment Advisors
- Discount Brokers
- Professional Money Managers

The range is from complete financial services, which includes investment research, to on line stock purchases.

Mutual Funds

The investor has another option, which is to invest in a mutual fund. Since its inception in the 1970s, it has provided an alternative for the investor who does not have the time, interest, or expertise to research stock picks. Today, there are as many mutual funds as there are stocks. The basic concept is that of pooling resources. A money manager with expertise in a given industry, investment style, or investment philosophy is identified. The manager determines the investment portfolio, including the asset allocation.

The investor measures their values in the form of Net Asset Value (NAV) shares. Mutual Funds are either load or no-load. You pay a fee at the front-end in load funds. In some no- load funds, you pay a back-end fee, known as a back-end loads. Some funds are open, which means you can purchase outstanding shares; while closed-end funds have a fixed number of shares, which are sold once. Closed-end funds are limited and could potentially sell at a premium.

While a management fee is charged to all funds, many charge a fee known as 12b-1. The 12b-1 fee represents expenses like marketing, broker's commissions, and advertising. The Securities and Exchange Commission is presently reviewing this fee.

When purchasing a mutual fund, it is important to answer the following questions:

- What are the investment objectives of the fund?
- What are the risk factors?
- What are the investment restrictions?
- What is the past performance?
- What are the costs and the fees?
- What is the background of the money manager?

Mutual Funds, continued

- What is the asset allocation, and how does it fit into my entire portfolio?
- What is the impact of any capital gains generated?

Mutual Fund Evaluation

There are third-party mutual fund evaluators and research sources; The following is just a handful:

- Morningstar Mutual Funds
- Value Line Mutual Fund Survey
- Standard and Poor's/Lipper Mutual Fund Profiles
- Investor's Guide to Low Cost Mutual Funds

Internet research is very much encouraged for all investors at every level.

Real Estate Investments

Investments in real estate are generally considered a hedge against inflation. Real estate investments may be held in the following forms:

- Residential Property
- Income-Producing Properties
- Syndicates and Residential Partnerships
- Real Estate Investment Trusts (REITs)

Precious Metals

Gold is generally considered a hedge against inflation. When held in bars and bullion coins, gold is rather liquid and requires insurance, assaying, and safe storage. However, there are mutual funds and equities in the gold market with a range of risks and returns.

Art, Antiques, and Collectibles

This is a specialized form of investing and highly subject to market demand, which may be eclectic.

Trading Places

Securities are traded on various Markets:

- NYSE (New York Stock Exchange)
- AMEX (American Stock Exchange)
- NASDAQ (National Association of Securities, Dealers and Automation Quotations)

The top two exchanges are located in New York City. NASDAQ is automated.

Investing - Buying Stock or Mutual Funds

Dollar Cost Averaging

One of the best ways to invest is by dollar cost averaging. This is a method which allows an investor to capture the highs and lows of the market. It is recommended that an investor determine a monthly amount to invest such as $100, and invest monthly.

By dollar cost averaging, the investor benefits in the following ways:

- Buy more shares when the price is down.
- Slow down investing, if it looks too volatile.
- Buy fewer shares when prices are high.

Measuring Market Direction by Indexes

Many young investors look at the bottom line of their investments and determine the success of the investment based upon it. However, it is important for the investor to look not only to the bottom line, but to examine the components of that bottom line by evaluating the investment in relationship to its corresponding index.

Specifically, there are indexes, which comprise a series of categorically similar stocks, or bonds, which help the investor, set benchmarks. Each index covers a different sector of the market:

For example:

Index	Composition
Dow Jones Average - Industrial Average - Transportation Average - Utility Average - Composite Average	30 of the largest Industrials
Standard and Poor's 500 (Including NYSE and NASDAQ)	400 Industrials, 20 Transportation, 40 Utilities, 40 financials
AMEX Market Value Index	800 companies on the U.S. Exchanges
NASDAQ	Over-the-counter stocks
Value Line Index & **Wilshire 5000**	Blue Chip, Mid, and Small Caps
Russell 2000	Small Cap

Investors should research the index performance and determine their portfolio performance comparatively. The indexes set the general direction for how the investment in its class should be performing.

TAX PLANNING IS ESSENTIAL FOR INVESTMENT PLANNING

Investing in Tax-Deferred or Non-Tax-Deferred Vehicles

Tax-deferred vehicles allow the investor to accumulate earnings and capital appreciation without the burden of having to pay taxes first. Generally, tax deferrals are instruments for "retirement." Penalties are incurred if funds are withdrawn prior to age 59½.

Retirement options are as follows:

- Savings
- Individual Retirement Accounts (IRAs)
- 401(k)s
- Keoghs
- SEPs and SIMPLEs
- Money Purchase Plans
- Stock Bonus Plans
- Profit Sharing Plans
- Employee Stock Ownership Plans - ESOPs
- Defined-Benefit Plans

In order to smoothly and effectively transition into a "retirement" lifestyle, planning is necessary, in fact essential.

Workplace Wisdom Institute

Conclusion

The keys to investment planning are setting goals and objectives. One must "write the vision and make it plain so that he that reads it can run with it" (Habakkuk 2:2). Once the plan is written, research is required, determining risk and return is mandatory, and executing the plan is essential.

Practical Applications For The Investor

- Perform cash flow analysis. Do not just depend on a review of Net Operating Income (NOI) or projected income/earnings.
- Examine the fundamentals.
- In today's environment over the next 3 to 4 years it is reasonable to expect a return of 9 – 10%.
- During times of volatile market conditions, increase the equity in your home. In 2001, national residential values increased 8.34%, according to CNN.
- Remember, you are investing in the future of a company.
- Remember, debt is issued in the form of Bonds.
- Review Indexes to determine the direction you can expect in your investment performance.
- Never forget the value of the Law of Compounding Interest.
- Research is central to understanding investing.
- Determine your level of risk and return realistically to avoid disappointments.

You are not a serious investor until and unless you have your six-month Emergency Fund set aside.

Notes

Workplace Wisdom Institute

Investment Planning Appendix

Financial Profile

This self-scoring, step-by-step worksheet will help you identify the factors that influence the allocation of your investments, so you can reach your financial destination. The answers you provide will help to determine which investment vehicles are appropriate to get you there.

The questions deal with the money you are considering investing in a new account. The investment approach can vary from 100% fixed income to 100% equity. There are no wrong answers.

Just choose the best available answer for each question, and enter the corresponding point value in the square to the right. Adding up your total points will give you an indication of which investment portfolio strategy may be appropriate to meet your current needs. Remember, it is wise to review your answers with your investment professional. You always have the ability to invest more conservatively or aggressively than your worksheet suggests.

Thank you for taking part. Let’s begin. Pray and seek God's wisdom prior to answering any question. Be a Romans 8:14 person, "led by the Spirit of God."

How does this investment fit into your total financial picture?

1. Approximately what portion of your total "investable assets" – the dollar amount of the investments you currently have – will this investment represent?
(Use the formula below to quickly calculate your investable assets. Do not include your principal residence or vacation home when figuring this total.)

Less than 25% 8
Between 25% and 50% 7
Between 51% and 75% 3
More than 75% 2

Amount You Intend to Invest	**Total Investment Assets**				
$	$	=		x 100 =	

Points

Question 1. It is important to consider this investment in relationship to your total portfolio. The percent of your portfolio that this investment represents can make a difference in how conservative or aggressive you may want to be.

2. Which ONE of the following describes your expected future earnings over the next five years (assume inflation will average 3%)?

I expect my earning increases will far outpace inflation (due to promotions, new job, etc.) 5

I expect my earning increases to stay somewhat ahead of inflation 3

I expect my earnings to keep pace with inflation 2

I expect my earnings to decrease (retirement, part-time work, economically depressed industry, etc.) 1

Question 2. Your expectation for future earnings will help determine how your assets should be allocated. If you're expecting significant earning increases it may be appropriate to be somewhat more aggressive.

3. Approximately what portion of your monthly take-home income goes towards paying off installment debts (auto loans, credit cards, etc.) other than a home mortgage?

Less than 10% 8
Between 10% and 25% 6
Between 25% and 50% 3
More than 50% 1

Points

Amount You Intend to Invest	**Total Investment Assets**				
$	$	=		x 100 =	

4. How many dependents do you have? (include children you continue to support, elderly parents, etc.)

None 4
1 3
2-3 2
More than 3 1

Points

Questions 3 & 4 If a large portion of your income goes toward paying debts, you may need to have cash available in case of unforeseen circumstances. Or, you may have responsibility for ongoing family obligations. Either can dictate a more conservative approach.

Do you have other savings?

5. Do you have an Emergency Fund? (savings of at least six month's after-tax income)?	6. If you expect to have major expenses (such as college tuition, home down payment, home repairs, etc.) do you have a separate savings plan for these expenses?
No .... 2 Yes, but less than six months of after-tax income .... 6 Yes, I have an adequate Emergency Fund .... 8 **Points**	Yes, I have a separate savings plan for these expenses .... 8 I do not expect to have any such expenses .... 6 I intend to withdraw a portion of this money for these expenses. (Note: please answer question 12 accordingly) .... 5 I have no separate savings plan for these items at this time .... 2 **Points**

Questions 5 & 6 A six-month emergency fund helps protect you against unexpected events. Under unforeseen circumstances such as loss of income, many people need to draw on what was intended to be "long-term" money for short term needs. Unless you have separate savings for major expenses, you may have to use money from this investment. If you don't have an emergency fund, a conservative investment may be more appropriate.

What is your attitude toward risk?

7. Have you ever invested in individual bonds or bond mutual funds?	8. Have you ever invested in individual stocks or stock mutual funds?
No, and I would be uncomfortable with the risk if I did .... 1 No, but I would be comfortable with the risk if I did .... 9 Yes, but I was uncomfortable with the risk........ 2 Yes, and I felt comfortable with the risk .... 10 **Points**	No, and I would be uncomfortable with the risk if I did .... 1 No, but I would be comfortable with the risk if I did .... 15 Yes, but I was uncomfortable with the risk........ 3 Yes, and I felt comfortable with the risk .... 16 **Points**

Questions 7 & 8 Prior investment experience can help determine your attitude toward investment risk. If you have had experience with different investments and you are comfortable with the associated risks, you can better assess your risk tolerance.

9. Which ONE of the following statements describes your feelings toward choosing an investment?	10. If you could increase your chances of improving your return by taking more risk, would you?
I would only select investments that have a *low degree of risk* associated with them (i.e., it is unlikely I will lose my original investment) .... 2 I prefer to select a *mix of investments* with emphasis on those with a *low degree of risk* and a small portion in others that have a higher degree of risk that may yield returns .... 5 I prefer to select a *balanced mix of investments* with some that have a low degree of risk, others that have a higher degree of risk that may yield greater returns .... 9 I prefer to select an *aggressive mix of investments* with some that have a low degree of risk, but with *emphasis on others that have a higher degree of risk* that may yield greater returns .... 12 I would *only* select an investment that has a *higher degree of risk* and a greater potential for higher returns .... 16 Points	Be willing to take *a lot more risk* with all your money .... 16 Be willing to take *a lot more risk* with some of your money .... 12 Be willing to take *a little more risk* with *all* of your money .... 10 Be willing to take *a little more risk* with *some* of your money .... 5 Be unlikely to take much more risk .... 2 Points

Questions 9 & 10 Your comfort level with investment risk is important to how aggressively or conservatively you choose to invest. The comfort level you choose should be balanced with your desire to achieve your investment goals.

How long can you afford to tie up this money? (Time is a very important factor in determining your strategy for any single investment.)

11. In approximately how many years do you expect to need the money you're investing?	12. Do you expect to withdraw more than one-third of the money in this account within ten years (for a home purchase, college tuition, or other major need)?
Within 2-3 years .... 5 Within 4-6 years .... 25 7-10 years .... 40 11-15 years .... 45 More than 15 years .... 50 Points	No .... 50 If yes, when do you expect to withdraw from the account Within 3 years .... 5 4-6 years .... 30 7-10 years .... 50 Points

Questions 11 & 12 Determining the time frame for your investment is critical to making an investment decision. Over time, certain investment types outperform others. Historically, stocks outperform bonds and short-term investments over long periods. So the longer you're putting money away, the more important it is to place some in growth investments. Shorter-term money belongs in more conservative investments that are less subject to fluctuations. The longer your money can sit and take advantage of market cycles, the more aggressive you may want to be.

Total Points: Add up the points for all twelve answers

Points

Which type of portfolio should you consider?

Now that you've added up your total points for all twelve questions, simply match that number with the chart below. Please note that if you have a very short time frame, you may want to be more conservative than your point score suggests.

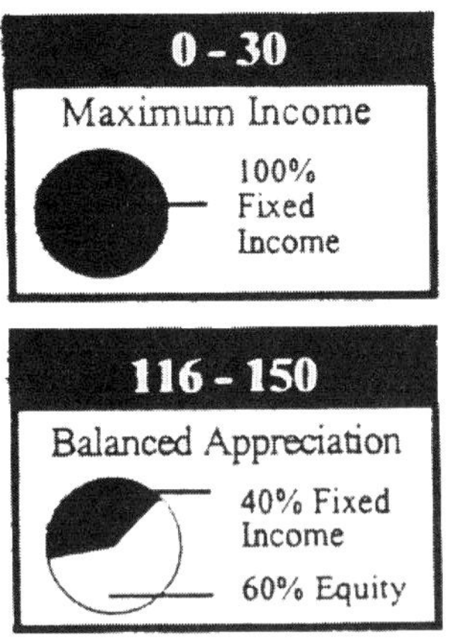

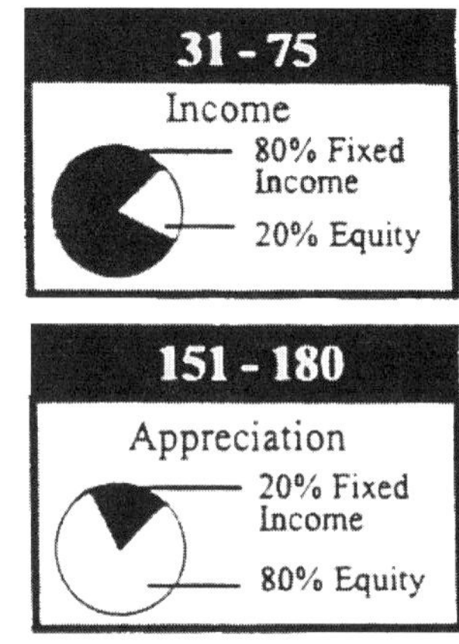

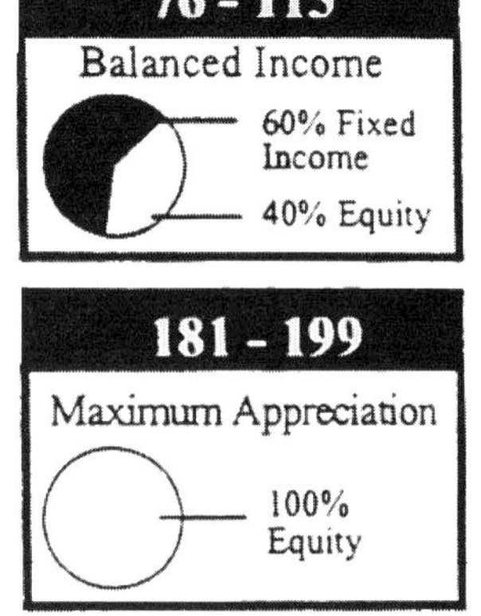

Additional Information: These questions will help you determine the specific strategy within your recommended portfolio.

13. Considering your tax bracket, do you prefer to use tax-exempt fixed-income investments even though tax-exempt investments may provide a lower current yield than equivalent taxable investments? (Circle one)

    Yes **No**

14. Diversified portfolios often include international investments. Are there any reasons why you would not want international securities as part of your portfolio? (Circle one)

    Yes **No**

For Your Next Steps, Consult Your Financial Advisor.

Remember, the asset allocation suggested by this score is meant to offer an example of the type of allocation you might want to consider, based on the average person with a similar score. The final decision on an asset allocation model is yours, based on your individual situation, needs, goals, and risk tolerance, which may include factors or circumstances beyond the scope of this worksheet. Furthermore, this example is based on your current assessment of these factors. If any of these factors should change, please review your investment strategy. At a minimum, you should review your allocation on an annual basis. For more complete information on any mutual fund, including charges, expenses, and applicable redemption fees, call your Financial Advisor. Read everything carefully before you invest or spend your money.

Asset Allocation Portfolios

Asset Class	Asset Allocation	Maximum Return	Minimum Risk
Model	*Goal*	*Fund Mix*	*Appropriate for Investors*
Maximum Income  Fixed Income 100%	Monthly Income	Long and intermediate term: Government bonds Corporate bonds	▪ Seek maximum monthly income ▪ Want a higher current yield
Income 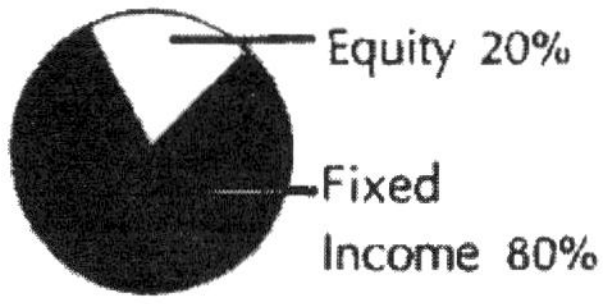 Equity 20% Fixed Income 80%	Stability of Principal	Long and intermediate term: Government bonds Corporate bonds Small stock component	▪ Intermediate term goals with stable monthly income ▪ Want to protect investment yet have hedge against inflation ▪ Equity outpaces inflation
Balanced Income 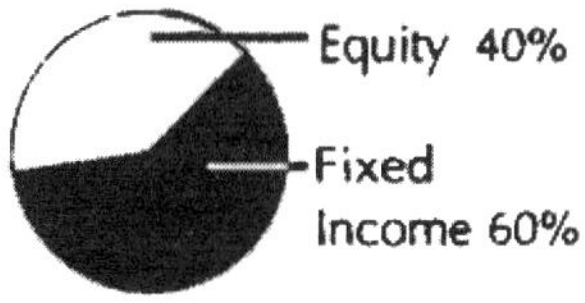 Equity 40% Fixed Income 60%	Growth and Current Income	Government and Corporate Bond funds Stock funds	▪ More stability than stocks alone ▪ Build capital and protect value of portfolio ▪ Seek moderate current income
Balanced Appreciation 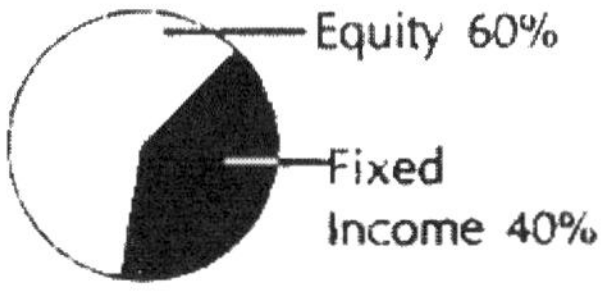 Equity 60% Fixed Income 40%	Growth and Current Income	Stock funds Government and Corporate Bond funds	▪ More stability than stocks alone ▪ Seek moderate current income ▪ Build capital, understanding moderate portfolio swings
Appreciation 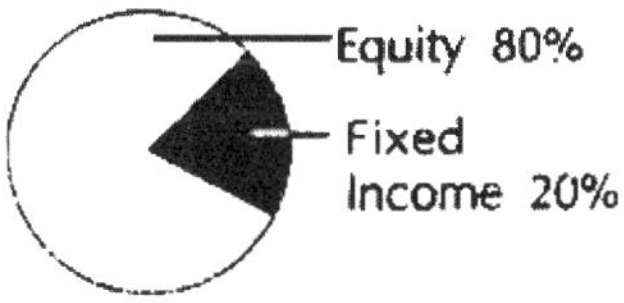 Equity 80% Fixed Income 20%	Long-Term Growth	Stock funds Government and Corporate Bond funds	▪ More interested in outperforming inflation ▪ Less concerned with current income ▪ Wealth accumulation, understanding portfolio swings
Maximum Appreciation 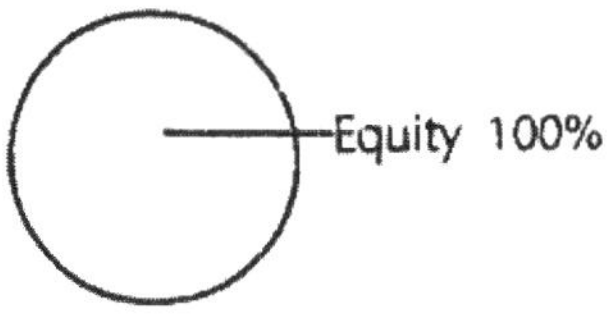 Equity 100%	Maximum Growth of Principal	Exclusive investment in Domestic and International Stock funds	▪ Weather frequent shifts in portfolio values ▪ Maximum growth of assets ▪ Seek highest potential returns

If you were to receive from an inheritance $100,000 tax-free, what dollar amounts would you spend in the next year in the following categories?

______________	*Gold, Silver*	______________	*Medical*
______________	*Recreation*	______________	*Dental*
______________	*Reduce Debts*	______________	*Precious Gems*
______________	*Bank Savings*	______________	*Automobile*
______________	*Commodities*	______________	*Buy own Home*
______________	*Bonds*	______________	*Treasury Bills*
______________	*Collectibles* *(Art, Antiques, Stamps, etc.)*	______________	*Charity*
______________	*Stock Market*	______________	*Church*
______________	*Money Market Funds*	______________	*Go into Business*
______________	*Vacation*	______________	*Give to Family*
______________	*Mortgages*	______________	*Mutual Funds*
______________	*Credit Card Debt*	______________	*Real Estate Investment Type Price*

(1)		(2)		(3)			(4)	(5)			(6)
52 Weeks					Yld		Vol				Net
Hi	Lo	Stock	Sym	Div	%	PE	100s	Hi	Lo	Close	Chg
$34\frac{3}{8}$	$21\frac{1}{2}$	XYZIndust	XYZ	.48	2.0	16	2542	$24\frac{1}{2}$	$23\frac{1}{4}$	$24\frac{3}{8}$	$+1\frac{1}{8}$

How to Follow Your Stock in the Newspaper
The Detroit Free Press

Stock listings may look like endless seas of incomprehensible figures, but they can be very useful sources of information. Here's a key to unlock their mysteries.

Note This fictitious example is based on the format of the Wall Street Journal and other major newspapers. Some publications may use abbreviated formats that carry only some of the items described.

1 The highest and lowest prices of the stock are shown for the last 52 weeks. These figures may give you an idea of the stock's price trend over the past year. Note that stock prices are given in fractions of dollars. The fraction ½ refers to 12½ cents. Therefore, 34 3/8 equals $34,375.

2 Company names are abbreviated, listed alphabetically and followed by the ticker symbol. Symbols are often related to the name of the company – XYZ for our fictitious XYZ Industries – but not alw**Error! Bookmark not defined.**ays. CHI, for instance is the symbol for Furr's/ Bishops Cafeterias.

3 "Ytd" stands for yield and "Div" for dividend. Yield, in general, is the return, in the form of dividends, on an Investor's capital investment. A dividend is a payment of a portion of a company's profits to its shareholders. Under "Div" you'll find the annual dividend disbursements per share based on the last declared payment by the company. If a company does not pay cash dividends, this column will be blank.

The column headed "%" gives you percent yield, or how much dividend you get for what you pay. This figure is calculated by dividing the dividend by the closing price (next-to-last column).
in this example, you could divide.48 by 24 3/8 to get 2.0%, the figure in the ""% column. The higher the figure, the more of your purchase price you will receive back in dividends each year.

Figures in the percent yield column vary widely; some investments, with high percent yields, are good for accumulating current income (income stocks), while other investments may pay off mainly in the form of capital gains (how much their stock prices increases over time). These are known as growth stocks.

"PE," or price-earnings ratio, is the relationship between the price of one share of stock and the annual earnings of the company. In this example, the price of an XYZ Industries share is 16 times the company's earnings per share for the most recent four quarters. As with percent yield, there is no perfect PE ratio. Some stocks that have accelerating earnings may have higher PE ratios; these are usually growth stocks. One the other hands, an income stock that pays consistently high dividends will tend to have a lower PE ratio.

"Ytd" stands for yield and "Div" for dividend. Yield, in general, is the return, in the form of dividends, on an Investor's capital investment. A dividend is a payment of a portion of a company's profits to its shareholders. Under "Div" you'll find the annual dividend disbursements per share based on the last declared payment by the company. If a company does not pay cash dividends, this column will be blank.

4 This column shows the volume of shares (In hundreds) traded on the previous day. For the true figure, multiply this number by 100. On the day before this report, 254,200 shares of XYZ Industries stock were traded. If a stock is underlined, it indicates an unusual sales volume that day.

5 "Hi," "Lo," and "Close" tell you a stock's highest, lowest and closing price for the previous trading day.

Other mysterious letters:
- ***pf*** alter a company's name indicates the information given is for preferred stock rather than common stock.
- ***s*** indicates a recent stock or company dividend within the last 52 weeks.
- ***B*** means this stock issue is (issued within the last 52 weeks), but this doesn't necessarily mean the company is new.

Notes

Estate Planning

The

Wealth Transfer

Estate Planning - The Wealth Transfer

A hallmark of the wealthy is their understanding of the importance of establishing a legacy by achieving in one's lifetime what is far too great to consume. So substantial is such a legacy that future generations are blessed with a great inheritance to carry on.

The wealthy have depth, which contrasts dramatically with the rich. Wealth suggests permanence, stability, and appropriate surroundings. Wealth is a state of being which encapsulates riches, prosperity, and affluence. Rich is a quantitative or qualitative word that describes possessions, resources, and production yields; for example, costly, abounding, elaborate, worth, expensive; high ratio, great value, and fine. Riches may represent possessions, which are newly acquired. Riches can be obtained over night, but wealth has a stream of history, a legacy of prosperity, and is characteristically in a class of its own.

A man or woman whose mind and life is committed to establishing a history beyond them has truly begun to understand Jesus Christ's purpose and intent in leaving one of the greatest legacies of all to the world: the New Testament.

The Word of God is full of instructions for handling money intergenerationally. Proverbs 13:22 tells us, "A good man leaves an inheritance to his children's children: and the wealth of the sinner is laid up for the just." (KJV)

Psalms 112:1-3 states, "Praise ye the LORD. Blessed is the man that fears the LORD, that delights greatly in his commandments. His seed shall be mighty upon earth: the generation of the upright shall be blessed. Wealth and riches shall be in his house: and his righteousness endures forever." (KJV)

If God's plan is for wealth and riches to be in the house of His people and He directs us to leave an inheritance for our grandchildren, then it is clear that ***God wants us to plan financially for at least three generations.*** Those who live positioning themselves to generate wealth inter-generationally are in the perfect will of God.

Estate Planning

The method, that has been provided for us to plan, is known as estate planning. A good estate plan assumes an orderly transfer of assets during one's lifetime, and most often upon death. The estate plan is established to fulfill the wishes of the deceased, to avoid taxes, and to maintain a legacy.

Just as Jesus took inventory of His assets and left His Last Will and Testament, we are called to do the same. In order to begin the estate planning process, you must know what you:

- Own
- Have an interest in
- Have incidence of ownership in

You must verify and have legal evidence of ownership and understand how the ownership is held. This could include titles, legal agreements, and knowing if the item or property is solely owned, jointly held, has multiple owners, etc.

You can see the importance of each component of the Financial Planning process and how each detail creates the master plan. The information of ownership can be gleaned from all of the other documentation prepared, as suggested in this manual.

One reason people do not complete an estate plan is because they fear death, dying, and everything related to the issue. However, we as Christians are blessed because we know we have a greater eternal inheritance in heaven, and we shall rule and reign in life with Christ Jesus. We also know that the things in this life are temporal.

The Word of God states that "every good and every perfect gift is from above," therefore, given the manifold blessings we have received from God, we are required to steward them even

Estate Planning, continued

after our departure from this life. If we are diligent to make preparations as a "faithful steward" then God will reward us ***in*** our own lifetime with more to steward. Many believers are missing the opportunity to increase because they are not being faithful with what they already have!

What Is An Estate?

The word "estate" refers to everything solely or jointly owned by a person. Upon death, the person's assets comprise what is known as an "estate of the decedent." The estate is generally amassed through outright ownership, a beneficiary, a trust, a contract, a business, or through current law. An estate generally includes the following:

- Business Interests and Investments
- Life Insurance
- Real Property (houses, land, etc.)
- Qualified Retirement Plans and Non-Qualified Retirement Plans (pensions, 401(k)s, annuities, etc.)
- Joint Interests (assets held with others)
- Personal Assets (cars, clothing, jewelry, etc.)
- Any other Asset Legally Owned or having Incidence of Ownership, not referenced above

Tax Implications – Net Estate Tax (Death Tax) and Gift Tax

After a person dies and their money, possessions, and other assets, that are to be transferred to other individuals, two taxes affect how much money each individual finally receives. Upon death, the U. S. Government is entitled to a death (estate) tax and a gift tax.

Estate Tax

The federal government for death tax purposes defines the Gross Estate. While provisions in the tax code are graduated based on the size of the estate, the tax ranges from 18% up to 50%. Yes, without proper planning, the taxman awaits at death's door-step. The following is the Federal Estate Tax Schedule.

The Federal Estate Tax is computed as follows:

1. Determine the Gross Estate.
2. Subtract from the gross estate the permissible deductions.
3. Add the value of taxable gifts made after 1976.
4. Apply the unified rate schedule to the taxable estate.

   The result is the tentative estate tax.

Next:

5. Subtract the tentative estate tax from any gift taxes payable (not actually paid) on post-1976 gifts.
6. Deduct the following applicable credits:
   - The unified tax credit
   - The credit for gift tax on pre-1977 gifts included in the Gross Estate
   - The credit on tax for prior transfers
   - The credit for foreign death taxes

   Result = Net Estate Tax Due

Workplace Wisdom Institute

The result is the net estate tax, which is due generally nine months after the death. The government does allow for a unified tax credit, which offsets the taxes owed. In 2002, the amount of the credit is $1,000,000. The credit acts to exempt the transfer of property from the estate taxes that results in a reduction in the amount of estate taxes owed. The use of the credit has to be planned, to maximize its ability to reduce taxes.

The estate tax potentially downsizes the amount of money that can be transferred to the heirs, which can be as much as 50% without estate planning prior to the death of the grantor.

The government requires that estate taxes be paid when assets are transferred from one individual to another. This is what's known as a taxable event. You can transfer any amount of assets to a spouse without being taxed (unlimited marital deduction). Without tax and estate planning, these taxes can be very substantial *and are required to be paid within 9 months.* For large estates, when there is no cash available it is recommended that money be secured through an insurance policy. This prevents you from having to sell the asset in order to pay the taxes.

Example

A widower dies and leaves his family house to his only son. He has no other assets. When the house was initially purchased 25 years ago, he paid $500,000. At death, its fair market value (FMV) is $2,000,000. The father transfers the house to the son but has made no estate plan provisions. The following is the impact.

The deceased father's estate pays taxes on the $2,000,000 in order for it to be transferred to the son.

Depending on the deductions and credits ($1,000,000 unified tax credit), the father's estate tax could be as high as 50%.

$2,000,000	Decedent's estate-house FMV
<$1,000,000>	Unified tax credit
$1,000,000	
$1,000,000	Net taxable estate
<$435,000>	Estate Tax (49% bracket on excess)

$435,000 in taxes are due to the government on behalf of the father's estate.

If the son does not have $435,000 to pay the taxes, the son must sell the house, or mortgage it to pay the deceased father's estate taxes.

If the son sells the house for more than $2,000,000, the son or father's estate pays more taxes on the capital gain.

Conclusion:

The son cannot keep the house, even though his father left it to him, unless the estate taxes (approximately $435,000) can be paid. The father should have provided for the proper transfer of his estate and payment of estate taxes prior to his death.

Gift Tax

Whenever an individual receives money or possessions from someone else valued at more than $11,000, the federal government assesses a gift tax. The gift must be reported on the individual tax return. The unified tax allows a person to gift up to $1 million dollars without taxable consequences.

It is important to take the gift tax into consideration when gifting to anyone other than a spouse. The godly report income, pay the tithe, and the taxes. Some people who are unfamiliar with tax laws assume they can spend all the money, but end up having large tax bills with no money to pay the tax bill, if the giver has not accounted for the taxes.

Example:
An inherited gift of $100,000 requires taxes to be paid at a rate ranging from 37% to 50%.

John Smith inherited, $100,000 from his rich uncle which transferred at death. Eleven thousand is considered a non-taxable gift and $89,000 is taxable. This could increase the tax bracket that John is in and cause his federal tax rate to increase by as much as 39.1%. This could result in John paying $34,799 in taxes. The cash he would receive is $65,201, if the uncle was over his unified tax credit.

The Rich Family Example

The Rich family read *Dominating Money,* tapped into God's supernatural economy, and became very rich. They are planning to convert their riches into wealth. James is 68, and his wife Mary is 62. They have two grown children, ages 42 and 38. Each of the children were blessed with two children, totaling four grandchildren. They are in the printing and graphics business.

The following reflects Mr. and Mrs. Rich's net worth and summarized personal financial statement.

Asset	Fair Market Value	10-year Increase @ 5% per year	Outstanding Debt	Ownership	Beneficiary
Cash	$100,000	$162,889		Joint (JT)	
Marketable Securities	$400,000	$651,558		JT	
House	$2,000,000	$3,257,789	$ 0	JT	
2nd House	$200,000	$325,779		JT	
Cars (3)	$100,000	Depreciated To $30,000	$ 0	2 Jim 1 Mary	
Art Collection	$200,000	$325,779	$ 0	JT	
Business	$2,000,000	$3,257,789	$500,000	Jim	Mary
Pensions	$1,500,000	$2,443,342			Mary
Total	**$6,000,000**		<$500,000>		
The Rich's Net Worth	**$5,500,000**				
Mary's Net Worth		**$ 10,454,925**	**$0**		

In the example above, Jim dies and transfers everything over to his faithful loving helpmate Mary. Jim's estate can transfer everything to Mary without tax consequences. However, upon Mary's death, all taxes are due if no plans have been made.

Mary's gross estate is in the 50% estate tax bracket. The federal government would like to take as much of the $10,454,925 as possible, up to 50%. Without estate planning, the Rich's have transferred a substantial amount of their legacy and godly inheritance to the government.

Proper planning should have been done prior to Jim's death. They could have begun to transfer assets to the children, to the grandchildren, and give to their church, which is tax exempt (from their estate) ***in Jim's lifetime***. They should have begun transferring and gifting while Jim was alive, so that the transfer would have significantly reduced their taxes. They would have obeyed God and left an inheritance to their children's children and been a blessing to their church by building the Kingdom of God and giving to the household of faith.

You can see why the process of Estate Planning is essential. If you truly believe you are going to the wealthy place, you need an Estate Plan!

What is an Estate Plan?

An estate plan is more than just a will; it is a thought-out plan of the distribution of one's assets for the purpose of ensuring for the needs of the family, reducing taxes and providing a legacy to the next generation or generations. This distribution generally begins with the departure of the owner; however, the more sophisticated and substantial the gross estate is, the sooner the process can begin — within one's own lifetime. This point is important for the body of Christ to understand as we go to the wealthy place.

An estate plan is necessary and required of every individual who owns something, no matter how much or how little. A plan of divestiture or disposal of assets is the Christian response to stewardship. When a person does not plan to transfer stewardship, s/he dies without regard for the consequences, which is not edifying to anyone, especially loved ones.

Estate Planning - The Wealth Transfer

Departure from this life without making the proper preparations can result in major problems. The potential consequences of dying without an estate plan include:

Dying Without an Estate Plan

- **The remaining family could become destitute**

  No money for funeral expenses

  Loss of income

  Loss of assets

  Tax liens for unpaid taxes

  No education for the children

  Loss of family residence

  Loss of family business

Other calamities:

- **Chaos in the family**

  Fighting over assets

  Lawsuits in the family

  Paternity claims

  There is no common law marriage in Michigan, since 1957.

Other Troubles:

- **Bankrupt Estate**

  Federal Estate Tax, up to 50%

  Dying insolvent (bankrupt)

  Inability to pay your last tithes

  Inability to pay outstanding bills

Dying Without an Estate Plan, continued

This manual deals primarily with components of an Estate Planning process including:

Wills

- Guardianship of Minors
- Ownership Issues
- Joint trusts
- Types of Trusts
- Powers Provided in Trusts
- Lifetime Gifts
- Gifting
  - a) To your children
  - b) To your Church
  - c) Generation-skipping Gifts (grandchildren)

Other Pertinent Estate Planning Issues

Wills

Every adult needs a will. The preparation of it should not be solely based upon the value of your assets. If you own anything, you need to prepare a will.

This is especially true if:

- You are a business steward
- You have a spouse
- You have children
- You desire to bless your church
- You steward (own) substantial assets
- You have desires that you want honored

A will is a list of detailed instructions, which are to be legally executed by someone (a personal representative) whom you designate. The will allows the decedent (recently departed) to dispose of their assets in an organized fashion. For a will to be legally binding, there are legal criteria for it to be valid. Once your will is legally created, you are called the testator.

The following conditions must be legally met:

a) By law, you must be of legal age, 18.

b) You must have a sound mind, (Testamentary capacity).

c) The will must conform to the state's will development requirements.

d) The will should be typewritten.

e) The will must have at least one clause outlining the plan for distribution of assets, which are the instructions.

f) You must appoint at least one executor, administrator, or personal representative.

Dying Without an Estate Plan, continued

g) You must date the will.

h) You must sign the will in the presence of two witnesses; a witness can be, but should not be, a beneficiary.

Many times people believe that they do not need a will because they don't have a lot of money. But we have seen families divided, divorced, and hurt deeply because of the lack of clarity in the disposition of assets, which in sum total, financially didn't amount to much but emotionally, was explosive.

Some people believe that, because they have designated beneficiaries or are in co-ownership relationships, this is sufficient. Not so. There are always assets that are forgotten about, that are left subject to the Probate Court. A Pour-Over will allows the decedent to capture all assets that were not transferred to the trust but were targeted for transfer into the estate trust.

Also, there are decisions that have to be made which can only be captured in a will. An example of this is:

- Guardianship of minor children

Dying Intestate (Without a Will)

Without a will, you are subject to the Probate Court and distribution as set forth by the state. The courts will appoint someone who you may or may not have wanted to handle your affairs. The same holds true for your children if they are minors. If you do not designate a guardian, one will be appointed. This could result in someone raising your children just for the money or, worse, by default, because you did not make the necessary legal provisions for their care.

Consequences Of Departing This Life Without A Will

Many people say "that would never happen to me," yet on average, seven out of ten people die without a will. This is astounding. The following are some of the consequences of not having a will:

- A surviving spouse may get as little as 1/2 of the husband's or wife's assets, the 1/2 remaining will go the children.
- For children under 18, their share is held and managed by the court until they become 18, at which time they get a lump-sum upon becoming a numeric adult.
- Someone whom you wanted to receive a portion of your assets may be disinherited.
- At this point, most of the taxes and administrative costs cannot be avoided or defrayed – it's too late.
- An Administrator is selected to handle your affairs by the judge of the Probate Court whose docket includes your case.
- Guardianship for children under 18 will be determined by the Probate Court.
- There is a prohibition on any gift being made to the church, other family members, or any charity– it's too late because the state laws determine distribution.

If many who have gone on were to look back and see the consequences of their lack of planning and stewardship, they

Consequences Of Departing This Life Without A Will, continued

would simply cry and be heart broken after having worked so hard to accumulate their assets, only for the state to be in control of them and government taxing their estate maximally.

Finally, every adult has a will. Either you prepared it or the state in which you live prepared it. But you do have one. If you die without a will, the state statues known as the laws of intestacy take over. In Michigan, the basic state distribution would be as follows for a person who died without a will:

$400,000 Estate	**$400,000 Estate**	**$400,000 Estate**	**$400,000 Estate**
Scenario A	***Scenario B***	***Scenario C***	***Scenario D***
Spouse w/2 kids by her	Spouse w/prior marriage kids his	Single w/ 2 children	Single w/no children
Spouse gets the first $150,000	Spouse gets the first $100,000	Children split $400K in half	Parents get $400,000**
Wife splits ½ the $250k with kids	Wife splits ½ the $300k w/his kids	Child 1& 2 get $200,000** each	No Parents Grandparents **
Each Child gets $62,500**	Children split $150,000**	If child is deceased, then grandchild	No grandparents, aunts, uncles No aunts and uncles, then cousins **
			No heirs, then all goes to the State

(The estate may be inclusive of a house, car, some insurance, and some cash).
** Taxes usually first paid by the estate.

Workplace Wisdom Institute

Estate Planning - The Wealth Transfer

This example shows statutory distribution. Assets can be passed to a spouse tax-free due to the marital deduction, which is unlimited. Other transfers, unless subject to the charitable contribution rules, are subject to taxes if they exceed the $1 million unified tax credit. This, too, can be managed if a planned transfer is made through a vehicle called a trust agreement, covered later in this section.

Practical Application

A few helpful points about the preparation of a will:

- Pray first, seek God's direction, work ***with*** your family, and walk in love.
- Assume that you died and went home to be with the Lord yesterday. What would you have wanted to take place with your assets? What is your desire for distribution?
- The size of the estate does not matter – key point.
- Seek legal counsel to prepare the will. If major assets are involved, never prepare the "home spun" will bought at the store.
- Use percentages instead of actual dollar amounts (Review and revise on a regular basis).
- Be realistic. Don't force things on people.
- Update the will at least every two to three years or upon a major life event (such as, birth, death, marriage, tax law changes).
- All of your affairs (documentation) must be in order, including those items which relate to the will.

Practical Applications, continued

- Prepare a letter of last instructions to say anything you might want to share. The nature of the letter may be spiritual (especially for unsaved loved ones), instructional, directional, and a keepsake for heirs.

- This is **not** the time to be ungodly (i.e., repay evil for evil, walk in unforgiveness, hurt people, act in pride, hoard, not be a blessing to your church and other ministries).

If you need to make changes in your will, which can occur from time to time, you must use a codicil, which is an instrument legally provided for making changes or alterations to the will. The will should be changed using the codicil, not by writing on the actual document, as these changes would be invalid. The document should not be altered except by the legal method described.

A copy of a comprehensive inventory and self-checklist is provided at the end of this section. Kenneth Copeland Ministries has graciously given us permission to include in our manual a comprehensive will with instructions and glossary. We have provided it for your review and possible drafting. We strongly recommend, however, that you consult an attorney for legal drafting of all of your documents.

Joint Ownership

The gross estate reflects those assets that the person has title to or has legal rights of ownership to.

There are states that treat assets as community property. Those states include Arizona, California, Idaho, Louisiana, Nevada, New Mexico, Texas, Washington, and Wisconsin. Community property means that both spouses own a separate, undivided, equal interest in the property. This means that both spouses have equal rights of ownership in the property, its earnings, salary, wages, compensation, etc.

In Non-Community Property States, there are three types of joint ownership, namely joint tenancy with right of survivorship, tenancy by the entirety, and tenancy in common.

Joint Tenancy with Right of Survivorship

- The owners are co-owners.
- At death, the property passes equally to the co-owners.
- Property passes directly; there is no probate involved.
- The decedent's ownership is included in the gross estate.

Examples of this type of ownership are jointly held bank or investment accounts.

Tenancy by the Entirety

- For the states that permit it, only married couples can only establish it.
- Neither spouse can dispose of any property without the other's consent.
- This type of ownership bypasses probate; however, it is included in the gross estate for the decedent.

Tenancy in Common

- A joint form of ownership in which several people maintain ownership. At death, the ownership transfers to the heirs, or designated beneficiaries, NOT to the other owners.

Tenancy in Common, continued

The manner in which properties or assets are held determines the options available for the transfer of the asset to another steward. One thing is certain, you cannot take it with you: therefore, a decision must be made to facilitate your desires being honored.

The Word of God states, in I Timothy 6:7, "For we brought nothing into this world, and it is certain we can carry nothing out". (NKJ)

TRUSTS

Trusts are legal entities (like corporations), which are created to house, manage, and ultimately distribute assets over the course of time. The assets are distributed based on the desires of the grantor. The trust must be funded, which requires assets to be titled in the name of the trust. Once titled in the name of the trust, the assets become known as the corpus, property, or principal of it. The beneficiaries of the trust can range widely from the spouse, to the children, to the church, and business associates.

Also, like a corporation, the trust has a life (determined by each state) and a purpose. One of its primary purposes is to eliminate or dramatically reduce estate taxes and protect your assets from Probate Court, thereby protecting your privacy. Secondly, it can hold assets for the length of time necessary for distribution, particularly when children are involved. Thirdly, it can effectively distribute assets to your church to reduce the estate and the associated estate taxes while maximizing contributions to do the Lord's work. Assets may be protected from creditors, not so with just a will. There are provisions for joint management of the assets, either through a financial institution or a trusted third party.

Do I Lose Control Of My Assets?

There are two types of Trusts: Revocable and Irrevocable. Revocable, also known as a Living Trust can be changed or dissolved at any time prior to death. The irrevocable trust, however, is sealed once executed. So, once the asset is placed in the Irrevocable Trust, control of the asset has been surrendered. The asset is now subject to the stated desires and plan upon death. There are very important uses for both types of trust entities. There are many different types of trusts, with a variety of uses.

Included in the trust agreement should be an article providing for a designated trustee. This is usually you during your lifetime and your designee upon your death. Upon your demise, or in the event of incapacitation, the powers are designated to whomever you believe will handle your affairs decently, and in order, and as you desire. *This must be a person whom you trust and have prayed about.*

Also included should be a separate document designating the Power of Attorney, which can be limited, to make certain decisions. This again, is someone whom you trust, have prayed about, and who is capable of making decisions in your stead and on your behalf.

Durable Power of Attorney allows the designated principal to function under all circumstances, including in the event of incapacitation or disability, because the powers are not limited. Durable powers allow for distribution, management, agent, and medical decisions on your behalf in the event of a disability wherein you are unable to function. It avoids going to court to secure guardianship or conservatorship.

Why Elect To Have A Trust?

The overwhelming reason is to avoid Probate Court and to avoid burdensome taxes. A revocable living trust is a private matter, which does not include the court system, which is a public forum. Therefore, a trust maintains the privacy of assets and distributions of the decedent. It avoids going to court to secure guardianship or conservatorship by allowing management during lifetime if disabled.

How Are Taxes Affected By The Creation Of A Trust?

During the trustee's lifetime, there are no federal gift taxes because the trust is revocable; there is no completed gift. This means that until and unless a distribution is made, there is no taxable event for the donor's estate or the gift recipient.

Federal Estate Tax

Federal estate tax is a tax on the transfer of property when a person dies. It is measured by the value of the property rights that are shifted by the decedent to others. This right to transfer property is taxed by the federal government up to 50% or half. The wealthy are faced with paying Uncle Sam or using trust vehicles to pass assets in the family and inter-generationally.

When large estates are involved, it is important to have tax advice because it may make sense to transfer all assets to the wife since the current stream of estate tax law and thinking is changing and may be of benefit when the second dies.

Pour-Over Will

This will in conjunction with the Revocable Living Trust allows all assets, which are not titled in the name of the trust, upon death to be "poured into the trust." This allows all the assets of the decedent to be placed into the trust for distribution.

Trust Vehicles For The Wealthy (And Not So Wealthy)

The following represents a few examples of the types of trust instruments available, including its purposes, and benefits. Since there is no downside to setting up a trust (the tax savings compensates well over the cost), we recommend that every believer have a trust and direct their assets.

Marital Deduction and By-Pass Trust

Through the use of the unlimited marital deduction (Trust) and the unified tax credit, taxes can be virtually eliminated or significantly reduced on the death of the first spouse.

The marital trust allows the surviving spouse to receive income and principal for life, and the right to designate the beneficiaries. The spouse does not receive the assets outright, because generally is the intent of the decedent that no taxable event occur which it would trigger tax consequence in the estate of the second to die. Upon the death of the second, the remainder, will pass to the children or others, and neither the husbands or wife's estate will owe federal estate taxes.

For estates over $1,000,000, gifting during lifetime is highly recommended. **Gifts are a major estate planning tool, particularly to charitable institutions, such as your local church. Such gifts reduce the amount of the gross estate for estate tax purposes.**

With the use of the unified tax credit, parents can plan to pass on amounts to their children in an amount equal to the credit.

Qualified Terminable Interest Trust (QTIP)

The marital deduction can also be obtained by putting qualifying property into a Qualified Terminable Interest Trust (QTIP), which will cause the assets to be eliminated from the first to die's estate. The surviving spouse can enjoy the income from such assets, but upon that spouse's death, estate taxes are due.
Oftentimes this option is used in second marriages with the intent to avoid taxes upon the first death.

Minor's Trust

Assets are provided for a child, should both parents die. The distribution is subject to the instructions of the parents, which may include disbursements over the course of the child's young adult life.

Generation Skipping Tax

Federal tax provisions have been made to discourage the transfer of assets to grandchildren or a third generation trust. The tax rate for transferring property by generation skipping is 50%. Planning is required to minimize this tax. The limit of transfer and thus exemption is $1,100,000 (2002). The tax is imposed in addition to the estate and gift tax on direct and indirect transfers to beneficiaries who are at least two generations younger than the transferor. The tax is burdensome, imposing, and ungodly! It penalizes those who have been blessed to go to the wealthy place and their heirs.

However, if you choose to transfer $1,100,000 or less, the amount is exempt from this tax. Planning must occur to maximize the distri bution of wealth while minimizing taxes.

Charitable Lead Annuity Trust (CLATT)

For estates that exceed the unified tax credit a CLATT can be set up to pay an income interest to a given charity of your choice. This could be an excellent alternative for gifting to the church, because the income is paid over a period of years. The assets are ultimately distributed to the designated heirs after the committed period of time has expired. This is an irrevocable trust, because control of the asset has been relinquished.

Charitable Remainder Trust

An individual, for example, makes a deferred gift to the church and still receives payments for life or a designated period. The advantage is that the asset is withdrawn from the estate with current income tax deductions. Typically, appreciating assets are

used in the transfer. As the asset appreciates the recipient (the church) has been greatly enhanced and the grantor has satisfied their desire to make such a contribution.

Life Insurance Trust

This trust, also called the Crummey Trust, is the repository of an insurance policy. Its purpose is to protect against gift and estate taxes. A life insurance trust can be used when a couple or individual faces estate tax in their generation and needs liquidity (cash) for its payment. It may be that the estate is so large that it behooves the wealthy person to absorb some of the taxes at the first death as part of the estate plan.

Qualified Domestic Trust

This is a method to handle the estate taxes for a non-U.S. citizen.

Grantor Retained Income Trust (GRITS), Grantor Retained Annuity Trusts (GRATS), and Grantor Retained Unitrusts (GRUTS)

In general, the purpose of these trusts is to allow the grantor to retain certain interest in the trust, with the remainder of the interest passing on to the beneficiaries. It is the intent that the giver retain and keep an interest income for a period of time, which is coterminous with the life of the donor; this can reduce the value of the gift. The hope is that the gift income would be exhausted at the same time as the life of the giver.

Professional Expertise

For all wills and trusts, a professional should prepare the documents. A lawyer with estate planning knowledge, background, and expertise within the state that you reside should prepare documents. Because of the importance of these documents, we strongly recommend and advise all readers of our material to seek professional help in the area of estate planning as the tax and estate laws change.

Wealth Preservation Trust

The Wealth Preservation Trust is a vehicle to manage or control the distribution to family members who have demonstrated their inability to handle money and operate without control or experience.

Closing Practical Applications in the Estate Planning Process

We can certainly learn from the mistakes of others so that we don't repeat them. The following are the common errors to avoid.

1. Ownership – Jointly Held Property

a. Potential for both state and federal gift tax

b. Lack of obtaining legal ownership

2. Improperly Arranged Life Insurance

a. No contingent beneficiary

b. Wrong beneficiary

c. Third-party beneficiaries (tax implications)

3. Lack of Liquidity

a. Not enough cash for final and on-going expenses

b. Federal Estate Tax shortfall

c. Federal and State Income Taxes (including pension distributions which have 15% excise tax if liquidated)

d. Payout for contributions (Not enough money to pay tithes and other contributions to the Kingdom of God)

e. Long-term care of the family (Not enough money)

4. Will Mistakes

a. Not up to date

b. Not valid

c. Wrong beneficiaries

d. No will

5. Wrong Selection of Executor

a. Incompetent, can't handle money

b. Conflict of interest (stands to personally benefit by decisions)

c. Can't manage affairs (disorganized, not thorough)

6. Left everything to spouse without proper tax planning

a. Second-to-die tax knock-out, leaving little for heirs

b. Lack of true planning (not taking the time necessary)

c. No charitable contributions (did not even pay last tithes and never considered gifting to the church but rather gave to the taxing authorities
- Federal Estate Tax
- Income Tax)

Closing Practical Applications in the Estate Planning Process, continued

7. **Lack of an Overall Plan**
    a. Lack of Generational Planning
8. **Lack of Tax Planning**
9. **Inadequate Records**
    a. Records that are not current
10. **Key Man Requirements In Business Unplanned**
    a. No buy-sell agreements
    b. No Succession Plan
    c. Uninformed spouse
11. **Improper Distribution Of Assets**
    a. Heir too young to handle inheritance
    b. Assets go to the wrong person
    c. Family never advised of the wealth-transfer strategy
    d. No letter of intent left to help family/distribution

12. **Lack of Financial Intelligence**

    a. Lack of understanding money

    b. Fear of numbers

    c. Lack of general understanding of investments

    d. Lack of general understanding of taxes

    e. Unwillingness to learn

    f. Not discerning the gift of God properly (wealth)

13. **No Estate To Distribute**

    a. Lack of accumulating assets to pass on

    b. Bankrupt estate (taxes unpaid, overwhelmed with debt)

14. **No Gifting to the Church - The Work of the Lord**

    a. Not considering your church in your estate gifting

    b. Allowing the federal government to eat your seed

    c. Not beginning gifting to the church in your lifetime

Conclusion

Planning your estate is very important, and we as believers are called by God to steward all the resources, assets, and blessings He has bestowed upon us. First Corinthians 4:2 tells us, "Moreover it is required in stewards, that a man be found faithful." (KJV)

Workplace Wisdom Institute

Notes

Estate Planning

The

Wealth Transfer

Appendix

Confidential Estate Inventory

Date ______________________

PERSONAL DATA

Client (Full Name) ____

Residence Address ______________________________ How Long? ____________

____ Telephone ______________

Business Address ______________________________ How Long? ____________

____ Telephone ______________

Occupation __________________________________ Social Security No. __________

Date of Birth ________________________________ Place (State) ____________

Date of Marriage _______________________ Spouse's Social Security No. __________

Dates of Service in Armed Forces: From _______________ To ____________________

Any disability? ___________(specify) ______% Monthly Pension $_________

Family and Other Dependents

Full Name	Relationship	Date and Place of Birth	Health

Other Advisors

Attorney: Name ____
Address ____
Telephone ____

Accountant: Name ____
Address ____
Telephone ____

Bank: Bank Name ____
Personal Contact ____
Address ____
Telephone ____

Remarks:

SELF-CHECKLIST

1. ( ) Have there been any changes in your family situation, since your will was drawn, that would necessitate revision of your will?

   ____

2. ( ) Where do you keep your will?

   ____

3. ( ) Who is the Executor of your estate?

   ____

4. ( ) Who drew up your will?

   ____

5. ( ) Who are the witnesses to your will?

   Name ________________ Address ________________

   Name ________________ Address ________________

   Name ________________ Address ________________

6. ( ) Are the witnesses to your will still living? ________________

7. ( ) Have you provided a sufficient amount of cash or other medium to meet all Debts, Taxes, Administration costs, and Cash Bequests, which your Executors must pay, without compelling them to sacrifice Estate of Business Assets?

   ____

8. ( ) Where are your business bank accounts?

   ____

9. ( ) Where do you keep the passbooks?

   ____

10. ( ) Where are your personal bank accounts?

    ____

11. ( ) Are any of these joint accounts? ______ With whom? ________________

12. ( ) Where do you keep the passbooks?

    ____

13. ( ) Where is your safe deposit box located?

    ____

14. ( ) Who else has access to it? Name ____
Telephone __________________ Where do you keep the keys to it?
____

15. ( ) Where do you keep your life insurance policies?
____

16. ( ) Have your Executor, Heirs, and Life Insurance Beneficiaries been advised to contact ___________________________ in the event of your death, to handle all details pertaining to the immediate settlement of your life insurance?

17. ( ) What is your Social Security Number? _________________________________

18. ( ) Where do you keep your Social Security Card? ____________________________

Notes:

ESTATE CASH FUND

Immediate Money Fund	Husband	Wife
(This fund is for the bills presented after death, which have to be paid.)	$________	$________

They may include:

- Medical & Hospital Expenses
- Burial Expenses
- Attorney's /Executor's Fee
- Federal Estate Taxes
- State Death Taxes
- Probate Court Cost

Debt Liquidation (Long term debt)	$________	$________

- Installment Loans & Credit Cards
- School and Auto Loans
- Unpaid Notes
- Outstanding Bills

Emergency Fund	$________	$________

(This fund is for unexpected bills not readily payable from current income.)
This includes:

- Major Repairs to Home or Auto
- Medical Emergencies
- Etc.

Mortgage Payment Fund (What would it take to pay off your mortgage today)	$________	$________
Child/Home Care Fund (To pay for the new expenses created as a result of the death of a spouse who formerly performed these duties without any cash outlay.)	$________	$________
Educational/Vocational Fund (The cost of training will vary by state and type of school)	$________	$________
Subtotal	$________	$________
Total Current Savings	$________________	
Total Liquid Assets	$________________	
Existing Life Insurance	$________________	
NEW CAPITAL REQUIRED	$________________	

SOCIAL SECURITY

Social Security Benefits are not paid automatically. They are paid only if applied for by the person entitled to receive them. The applicant must fill out proper claim forms, and substantiate the claim by furnishing necessary documents, and proof of statements as to age and other facts. The longer a person waits to secure some of these records, the more difficult it becomes, because the records themselves or witnesses become harder to locate with the passage of time.

The following is a list of important documents and records that should be assembled as soon as possible and carefully filed, preferably with your life insurance policies. These papers, and other documents, which will be needed immediately after death, should not be placed in a safe deposit box, but should be kept in a secure place where they will be available to the family or other beneficiaries.

I. Proof of Date(s) of Birth
   a. Yourself
   b. Your spouse
   c. Your children, if any
   d. Dependent parents, if any

   In any of the following forms:
   1. Birth certificate, or
   2. A duly certified public record of birth, or
   3. A duly certified church record of infant baptism, or
   4. Evidence from one or more of the following sources:
      a. A Bible or family record
      b. Certificate of naturalization
      c. Passport, etc.
      d. Military record

II. Proof of Marriage in any of the following forms:
   a. Marriage certificate, or
   b. A duly certified public record of marriage, or
   c. A duly certified church record, or
   d. Evidence from one or more of the following sources:
      1. Certificate of naturalization, or
      2. Citizenship papers, or
      3. Passport, etc.
      4. Military record

III. Cumulative Record of Employment and Wages (verified and brought up to date at least every three to four years)

IV. Discharge Papers – If a Veteran of the United States Armed Forces

In addition to the above, which can be assembled during lifetime, official proof of death (when that occurs) will have to be furnished as the basis for any application for survivor benefits. Claims for all benefits should be made at the nearest field office of the Social Security Administration, where applications and all other necessary forms are available. There, the claimant may secure, free of charge, any help he or she needs in making out the claim papers, including notary services.

The Christian Will Planning Guide of

Your Name ________________________________

Compliments of
Kenneth Copeland Ministries
Fort Worth, Texas 76192-0382

In the pages ahead, you'll be embarking on a very personal adventure... something no one else can do for you, something far more important than you probably realize. It's possible in fact, that what you're about to create in the following pages could have more impact on the Kingdom of God than you're able to imagine.

Remember for a moment the face of someone you love who is now with the Lord. You may not be able to remember the last words they spoke to you ... but suppose they had written a message to be given to you after they were gone. How would *those* words have affected you?

What you're about to fill out on these pages could be your final communication in this life to the people you cherish. Your words here, of faith, of love, of instruction, will affect their lives in ways you cannot even visualize.

That's why, as you approach these pages, you may feel a sense of awesome anticipation, even excitement. It's definitely appropriate. In fact, it's part of your unique heritage as a child of God. This world's children may tremble and quake inside when they look past this life to the next kingdom. But children of the Most High simply can't suppress that surge of exhilaration in knowing what awaits them.

So in the moments ahead, you are very likely to feel what any faithful servant of God would experience as you prepare your statement of triumph and faith and your ultimate declaration of love for the God who loves you.

Father,

"I come to You awed by the opportunity of creating in these pages something that will affect lives here on earth even when I myself am standing at Your throne"

"You alone, Lord God, fully realize how far reaching will be the impact of what I write here. I, therefore, submit myself totally to Your leadership. And I ask You right now to give me Your wisdom."

"Holy Spirit, guide me by Your power as I move through these pages that every detail outlined here will bring glory to the Father-and the love of Jesus to as many people as possible."

"May every word and every instruction shine with the light of Christ Jesus as I create my own Last Will and Testament to the glory of God, in Jesus' name. Amen."

MAKING A WILL IS AN ACT OF CHRISTIAN STEWARDSHIP

The earth is the Lord's, and the fullness thereof, the world, and they that dwell therein (Ps. 24:1).

The Bible has much to say about stewardship. Every Christian has been called by God to be a good steward over everything, which He has provided: family, finances, abilities, time, and material possessions. The faithful Christian steward acknowledges God's ownership of all things and his own responsibility to God for what he does with the things God has entrusted to him.

Isaiah, the prophet of God, said, *Thus saith the Lord, Set thine house in order; for thou shalt die.(2* Kings 20:1)

Unless Jesus returns, we know that death is a bridge which each of us must cross. The good steward knows that he is to keep his house in order at all times. A major part of keeping your house in order is to have an up-to-date, properly prepared will, which directs the disposition of your estate. It has been said that you can tell more about a man by reading his will than by reading his obituary. His obituary reveals only what the world thought of him. His will reveals the intent of his heart.

Most people acknowledge that they should have a will, yet polls indicate that only about 20 percent actually do have wills. Whether this indicates a fear of facing the inevitability of one's own death, ignorance, or slothfulness, the result is the same - an opportunity to be a good steward before God was lost by those who die without a Christian Last Will and Testament.

Stewardship is not just for the wealthy; it is for every Christian. When you total your assets, if you are like most people, you will find you have much more than you thought. Regardless of what you have, you need a plan. If, in truth, you have only a spouse, and/or children, you need to make your wishes known for them through a properly executed will.

THE STATE'S WILL FOR YOU

In the event you are a parent(s), and die, without your specific instructions, the court may direct that your children be raised in the home of a relative who may not offer the type of child rearing you desire. Or, the court may direct that they be placed in an institution. Without your specific instructions in a will, the courts assume the responsibility, which is rightfully, and legally yours.

Even though 80 percent of the people have never sat down with their attorney and prepared a will, they do have one. It has been prepared for them by their state legislature, and it will become effective through a court appointed administrator at the time of death. The state's will for you divides your assets according to a fixed pattern of priorities set by law, and which may not in any way reflect your desires.

Loved ones, your church, Christian ministries, and deserving friends will probably be left out. A disproportionate amount of your estate may go unnecessarily for taxes, surety bonds, and other estate expenses, which can be avoided through a properly drafted will.

If you die intestate (without a will), your spouse may have to petition the courts to get money for household expenses until the estate is settled Your good intentions, even if they are known, have no legal weight in the disposition of your estate unless they are available in the form of a written will.

CHRISTIAN TESTIMONY

Through his will, the Christian can testify to the Lordship of Jesus Christ. The provisions he makes in his will can be tangible proof of his Christian love for his family and others. Through it, his witness can live after him and bear fruit for years to come

Through your will, you have the ability to continue your Christian witness to the world after you die, and even to multiply it, through the lives you will be influencing for Christ long after you have gone home to be with the Lord. It is very important to have your will prepared by an attorney thoroughly familiar with the laws of your state. It is also important that your will be written when your mind is clear, your body sound, and your heart yielded to God.

MAKING A WILL IS SIMPLE...

Follow These Steps

1. Complete the following pages in this Planning Guide as fully as possible.

2. Select a trusted attorney and make an appointment with him as soon as possible. The attorney's fee for writing a legally conforming will is small in comparison to the estate savings effect of the will.

3. Take this completed Planning Guide to your attorney. He will draft your will in proper legal form according to your wishes.

4. If you have a will that is out of date due to changes in family relationships, changes in your estate, or in which you now wish to include a Christian bequest, take the out-of-date will with you to your attorney.

5. File your will in a safe place where it cannot be lost or accidentally destroyed. Advise your executor and first alternate executor of its safekeeping location.

6. If you have blessed your church ______________________, they would appreciate learning of the bequest. Please send the church a copy of the will. Ask them to hold it in the strictest confidence. If you are not comfortable with that, simply advise the church of your intentions.

PLEASE PRINT OR WRITE LEGIBLY.

This organization does not engage in rendering legal or tax advisory services. For advice and assistance in specific cases, the services of an attorney or certified public accountant should be obtained. The purpose of this guide is to bring to your attention the importance of having a will.

FAMILY STATUS

Legal Name ______________________________, ________________________, ________________________
Last First Middle

Permanent Address ____
Street City County State Zip

Date of Birth ____________ Social Security # __________________ Telephone # ______________

( ) Single ( ) Married ( ) Widowed ( ) Separated ( ) Divorced & Remarried

Legal Name of Spouse (if married) ____________________, ______________, ______________
Last First Middle

Permanent Address (if different from above)

____

____

Spouse's Date of Birth______________ Spouse's Social Security # ____________________

If divorced or widowed, please list name and address of former spouse.

____

Is title of any property owned by or with former spouse now in your name only? Give details: __________

____

Do you have a will now in force? ( ) Yes ( ) No. If yes, please attach a copy

Names of living children, deceased children, and legally adopted children. If no children, please list living parents and/or brothers and sisters.

Name	Relation	Birth Date	Address

WHERE APPLICABLE, ADDITIONAL INFORMATION ON YOU

Other names used by you ____

Any prior marriages? [ ] Yes [ ] No

Did prior marriage end in divorce? [ ] Yes [ ] No

Date Ended (month, day, year) ______________________________

Place Ended (city, county, state) ______________________________

Court Name (see divorce decree) ______________________________

Did prior marriage end in death? [ ]Yes [ ]No Date of spouse's death (month, day, year) ______________

Place of death (city, county, state) ______________________________

Children by prior marriage, if any, name

Name	Relation	Birth Date	Address

WHERE APPLICABLE, ADDITIONAL INFORMATION ON YOUR SPOUSE

Other names used by you ______________________________

Any prior marriages? [ ]Yes [ ]No Did prior marriage end in divorce? [ ]Yes [ ]No

Date Ended (month, day, year) ______________________________

Place Ended (city, county, state) ______________________________

Court Name (see divorce decree) ______________________________

Did prior marriage end in death? [ ]Yes [ ]No Date of spouse's death (month, day, year) ______________

Place of death (city, county, state) ______________________________

Children by prior marriage, if any, name

Name	Relation	Birth Date	Address

CHRISTIAN TESTAMENTARY SAMPLE A

THE STATE OF ______________________

KNOW ALL MEN BY THESE PRESENTS:

COUNTY OF ________________________

That, I __________________________, mindful of the brevity of this life, do herein make the following
Your name

statement of faith:

I believe in one God, Father, Son, and Holy Spirit, Creator of all things.

I believe that the Lord Jesus Christ, the only begotten Son of God, was conceived of the Holy Spirit, born of the Virgin Mary, was crucified, died, buried, resurrected, ascended into heaven and is now seated at the right hand of God the Father and is true God and true man.

I believe the Bible in its entirety, to be the inspired Word of God and the infallible rule of faith and conduct.

I believe in the resurrection of the dead, the eternal happiness of the saved, and the eternal punishment of the lost.

I believe in personal salvation of believers through the shed blood of Jesus Christ.

I believe in sanctification through the Word of God and by the Holy Spirit, and I believe in personal holiness, purity of heart and life.

I believe in divine healing through faith in the name of Jesus Christ and that healing is included in the redemption.

I believe in water baptism, in the Baptism in the Holy Spirit as distinct from the new birth, in speaking with tongues as the Spirit of God gives utterance (Acts 2:4), in the gifts of the Spirit, and the evidence of the fruit of the Spirit. I believe that all of these are available to believers.

I believe in the Christian's hope, the soon coming, personal return of the Lord Jesus Christ.

I believe in evangelism and missionary work in accordance with the Christian commission (Matt. 2:19).

I direct my Executor to photocopy this statement of faith and distribute it to each of my heirs because of my love for them and my desire for their eternal salvation

ARTICLE I

I, _________________________, of the County of ___________, State of ____________________
Your Name

being of lawful age and of sound and disposing mind and memory, do hereby make, publish, and declare this to be my Last Will and Testament, and do hereby revoke any and all other wills, codicils, and other testamentary paper heretofore made by me.

CHRISTIAN TESTAMENTARY SAMPLE B

THE STATE OF ___________________

KNOW ALL MEN BY THESE PRESENTS:

COUNTY OF _____________________

That I, ____, of the County of ___________________, State
(your name)
of _______________, mindful of the brevity of this life, and having placed my faith and confidence in Jesus Christ, my Savior and Lord, who redeemed me through His shed blood and death upon Calvary's cross for my sins and who, through His resurrection, assures me of eternal life, do hereby make, publish, and declare this to be my Last Will and Testament.

CHRISTIAN TESTAMENTARY SAMPLE C

THE STATE OF ____________________

KNOW ALL MEN BY THESE PRESENTS:

COUNTY OF _____________________

That I, ____, of the County of ___________________, State
(your name)
of ________________,

(Write Your Own)

CHRISTIAN TESTAMENTARY SAMPLE D - CONCLUDING ARTICLE

As a matter of personal testimony, I wish to state I believe the greatest possession that I have to leave my survivors is made up of my love for them, for the precious memories, and appreciation that I hold for them all, and further to repeat for them the fact that I believe their greatest inheritance, as well as my own, is the presence of God in our lives, His help to all of us, and to encourage my precious loved ones to always love God and to lean upon Him in times of any need and to live for Him throughout their lives.

"PERSONAL EFFECTS" BEQUEST'S

Many states allow the distribution of personal effects through additional pages added to the will. In order to do this, a statement in the Last Will and Testament should be similar to:

> *It is my intention to make a list of certain items of personal effects, which I would want to be distributed by my Executor to a designated person. In the event such a list is placed with this will, which list is wholly in handwriting, signed, and dated by me, then said list is specifically incorporated into this will by reference and my Executor shall make distribution of the designated items on said list as they are set forth. The bequests set forth on such list shall take precedence over any other bequest of disposition set forth herein.*

Notice that the statement is on "Personal Effects" and therefore excludes real estate and other specific bequests. The added page(s) is not a codicil. The personal effects page(s) is valid in most states because; the above "intention" is included in the properly executed will. Discuss with your attorney items that may or may not be listed according to your state laws.

The personal effects page must (1) be in your handwriting, (2) contain no erasures or corrections, and (3) be signed and dated.

The personal effects page heading should begin along the following lines:

> *As provided for under Article __________ of my Last Will and Testament, I make the following specific gifts and bequests:*

You may wish to verify this wording with your attorney. The actual bequests would then follow.

Example (all would be in your handwriting)

As provided for under Article 2:02 of my Last Will and Testament, I make the following specific gifts and bequests:

To my daughter, Jane Doe Smith of Dallas, Texas, I give and bequeath all my for jewelry, costume jewelry, and fur coat if she survives me by thirty days,

To John Doe Smith of Dallas, Texas, I give and bequeath my 1985 Ranger Boat, serial number 1269, 1985 Johnson Outboard Motor, serial number 3578, and 1985 Roadmaster Trailer, serial number 9621 if he survives me by thirty days.

Your Signature
Month, Date, Year
(Attach to Last Will and Testament)

WHAT DO YOU HAVE TO WILL?

AN INVENTORY OF YOUR ESTATE

I. PERSONAL PROPERTY

A. Household furnishings, furniture, books, musical instruments, autos, collections, etc. List items for special consideration. Others may be grouped.

Item	Approximate Value
	$
	$
	$
	$
	$
	$
TOTAL APPROXIMATE VALUE	$

B. Cash (Checking Accounts)

Bank	Address	If Joint Account, With Whom?	Amount
			$
			$
TOTAL IN CHECKING ACCOUNTS			$

C. Savings Accounts

Bank, Bldg. & Loan, etc.	Address	If Joint Account, With Whom?	Amount
			$
			$
TOTAL IN SAVINGS ACCOUNTS			$

D. Stocks, Mutual Funds, and Bonds (Government or other)

Item	Approximate Value
	$
	$
	$
	$
	$
	$
TOTAL IN STOCKS, MUTUAL FUNDS AND BONDS	$

E. Money Invested in Mortgages and personal loans

Item	Address	Approximate Value
		$
		$
		$
		$
TOTAL INVESTMENTS		$
Total Approximate value of all PERSONAL PROPERTY (add items A, B, C, D, and E)		$

INVENTORY (continued)

II. REAL PROPERTY (Real Estate and Buildings)

Type of Property	Address	If Owned Jointly, With Whom?	Value
			$
			$
			$
			$
TOTAL APPROXIMATE VALUE OF REAL PROPERTY			$

III. INSURANCE AND ANNUITIES

Company	Type of Policy	Beneficiary	Amount
			$
			$
			$
			$
TOTAL VALUE OF INSURANCE AND ANNUITIES			$
TOTAL ASSETS (Add Personal Property I, Real Property II, and Insurance III)			$

IV. APPROXIMATE DEBTS AND MORTGAGES AGAINST YOUR ESTATE

Debt or Mortgage to Whom?	Address	Value
		$
		$
		$
		$
		$
		$
TOTAL APPROXIMATE INDEBTEDNESS		$
Total Approximate value of all PERSONAL AND REAL PROPERTY AND INSURANCE, LESS TOTAL INDEBTEDNESS (IV – V = VI)		$

ESTATE PLANNING INFORMATION

Your Name ____
Last First Middle

Spouse's Name ____
Last First Middle

Address ____
Street City State Zip Code

Telephone Numbers: Home (____) __________________ Business (_____) ____________________

RETIREMENT PROGRAMS

Beneficiary	Source	Value Per Month Or Year

PLANNING OBJECTIVES

Check Only Those That Apply

( ) Assure the financial security of spouse __________, children __________________
( ) Provide for the education of children ____________, grandchildren _____________
( ) Provide for the support of persons other than immediate family members
( ) Provide for a final tithe (%) after fulfilling financial responsibilities to family
( ) Reduce costs of administration (avoid probate)
( ) Reduce Estate Taxes
( ) Reduce Income Taxes
( ) Reduce Capital Gains Taxes
( ) Assure adequate estate liquidity
( ) Increase spendable lifetime income
( ) Increase retirement income
( ) Assure retention of business in family
( ) Increase lifetime Christian giving without jeopardizing family's financial security

AUTHORIZATION

You are authorized to freely discuss the financial affairs of the undersigned with any of my professional advisors but with no one else. My attorney is further authorized to supply my church ministries ____________________ with copies of all Will, Trusts, and supporting documents to be prepared by him.

The above is approved as the personal objectives and desires of the undersigned.

Dated the _______________ day of ________________________, 20 ____.

SIGNED: ____

SIGNED: ____

HOW DO YOU WANT YOUR ESTATE TO BE DISTRIBUTED?

I. **Disposition of Estate if Spouse Survives**

Reciprocal wills bequeath entire estate to the surviving spouse? [ ] Yes [ ] No

Other ____

____

____

____

II. **Disposition of Estate if Spouse Does Not Survive**

A. Specific Bequests

You do not need to describe every item of your personal or real property in your will. Only if there is some specific item or property that you want to go to) a certain individual do you list it. And if you wish to leave a specific sum of money to a person, church, or ministry, you should stat the name and the amount.

Person or Organization	Relationship	Address	Property, Article or Dollars

B. Residuary Estate Bequests

After specific bequest and debts against your estate are paid, a residuary estate consisting of whatever s left will remain. This is usually disposed of on a percentage basis, as it is usually as possible to determine exactly what this amount will be. For example, four people, churches, or ministries could be remembered for 25 percent of the residue each, or, five for 20 percent, etc.

Person or Organization	Address	Amount of Percentage

NAMING AN EXECUTOR

An executor or executrix must be named and an alternate should be named in the event your first choice is not able or declines to serve. An executor should be someone whom you trust and who knows your affairs. It is his responsibility to see that the terms of your will are carried out according to your instructions. For those who die Intestate (without a will), the court may appoint an administrator or executor whom you or your heirs would not have chosen. It is definitely to your advantage to choose whom you wish to take care of this most important handling of your affairs. (You may have a third or fourth alternate.)

Executor ____

Last Name First Middle

____

Street City State Zip Code Relationship

Alternate Executor ____

Last Name First Middle

____

Street City State Zip Code Relationship

Final executor or trustee: In the ever, that none of the executors named above are able to serve, it is often advisable to name a major bank or trust company to serve as final choice for executor or trustee.

________________________	________________________
Bank of Trust Company	City, State, Zip Code

PROTECT YOUR. CHILDREN - NAME THEIR GUARDIAN

If you have minor children, a guardian should be named in the will. Appoint the one you wish to take care of your children until they are of legal age if both parents are deceased. If you do not feel the guardian is capable of handling the finances belonging to the children, then a separate trustee may be named to be responsible for administering the assets of the estate until the children reach legal age. This trustee would have no personal responsibility for the day-to-day care of minor children but would have economic control over the funds. If trusts are to be created for the benefit of minor children, it is sometimes advantageous, for reasons of continuity of management, to appoint the same person as executor and trustee.

Guardian for Minor Children	Relationship to Testator	City, State, Zip Code
Alternate Guardian for Minor Children	Relationship to Testator	City, State, Zip Code
Name of Trustee or Estate	Relationship to Testator	City, State, Zip Code

COMMON DISASTER CLAUSE

A remote possibility to plan for is when a husband and wife or heirs die in a common disaster or in close proximity in time. To cover this remote possibility, a common disaster clause, also called a simultaneous death clause, should be included in your will. Although two examples are given below, please discuss the importance of this clause with your attorney.

Example 1: If any beneficiary and I should die in a common accident or disaster, or if any beneficiary dies within days of my death, then all the provisions of this will; hall take effect as if such beneficiary had in fact predeceased me.

Example 2: In the event that any beneficiary, under this my will and I shall die under such circumstances that there is no sufficient evidence that we died otherwise than simultaneously, such beneficiary shall be deemed to have predeceased me.

Common Disaster Distribution ____

LAST CAN BE EVERLASTING

Through your Last Will and Testament, you can leave a legacy or bequest that will have everlasting effects. A legacy or bequest to your church will help insure the spreading of the uncompromised Word of God to millions of people worldwide.

A. Specific Bequest

I give and bequeath the sum of $______________ to my church be used in carrying on the purposes of said corporation. The receipt of the said corporation shall sufficient discharge to my Executor for the same.

B. Residuary Bequest

All the rest, residue, and remainder of my estate, real, personal, and mixed, which shall belong to me or be subject to my disposal or appointment by will, where ever situated, I give, devise, and bequeath, to my Church, a nonprofit corporation established by the laws of the State of Texas, to be used in carrying one purposes of said corporation. The receipt of the said corporation shall be sufficient discharge my Executor for the same.

SPECIAL INFORMATION

Please use this space for any additional information you wish to give to your attorney, explaining any testamentary trusts or any other desires not expressed in the foregoing information.

____

____

____

____

____

____

____

____

____

____

YOUR ATTORNEY

The foregoing pages of information are my desire concerning my Last Will and Testament. It is my wish to have my will drawn according to these instructions. If a bequest to is included, please send a copy of my will to the Christian Financial Planning Department.

Signed ____________________________________ Date ________________

PROFESSIONAL ADVISORS

My Minister

Name Street

City State Zip Code

My Attorney

Name Street

City State Zip Code

My Insurance Agent

Name Street

City State Zip Code

My Accountant

Name Street

City State Zip Code

My Banker or Trust Officer

Name Street

City State Zip Code

My Broker

Name Street

City State Zip Code

My tax records are located

Name Street

City State Zip Code

My safe deposit box is located

Name Street

City State Zip Code

My will is located

Name Street

City State Zip Code

GLOSSARY

Abatement: A proportional reduction of a debt or legacy due where the fund or the estate is insufficient to meet full payment.

Administration of Estate: Supervision by an executor or administrator. Management of the estate by an independent executor. Normally involves the collection, management, and distribution of an estate, including the legal proceedings necessary to satisfy claims of creditors next of kin, legatees, or other parties who may have any claim to the property of a d ceased person.

Adminstrator lAdminstratrix: In probate practice, a person to whom letters of administration, that is, an authority to administer the estate of a deceased person, have been granted by the proper court. An administrator resembles an executor, but, being appointed by the court in and not by the deceased, he has to give security for the due administration of the estate by entering into a bond with sureties called an administration bond. Administrator refers to a male and administratrix to a female.

Attestation: The act of witnessing an instrument in writing at the request of the party making it and subscribing as a witness.

Beneficiary: One for whose benefit a trust is created; a person having the enjoyment of property of which a trustee, executor, administrator or other has the legal possession; a person to whom a policy o insurance is payable.

Bequest: A gift of personal property.

Codicil: Addition to or qualification of one's Last Will and Testament.

Competent Witness: A person who, at the time of attesting to a will, could legally testify in court to the facts of which he attests by subscribing his name to the will.

Conservator: A guardian protector, preserver generally appointed by a court to care for the property of another.

Decedent: A deceased person, especially one who has recently died.

Descendant: One who is descended from another, a person who precedes from the body of another, such as child, grandchild, to the remotest degree.

Devise: A gift of real property by will; a devisor devises real property to a devisee and the disposition is tanned a devise.

Disposing Memory: On in which a person can recall the general nature, condition, and extent of property and his relations to those to whom he gives and to those from whom he withholds that property.

Distribution: Historically this meant title to the Intestate decedents personal property vested in his personal representative who subsequently distributed it to the interstate's distributees or next of kin, after the administration of the estate, which was the collection, and preservation of the decedent's personal property and the payment of his creditors.

Domicile: That place where a person has his/her true fixed and permanent home and principal establishment and to which whenever he is absent he has the intention of returning.

Escheat: In American law, a reversion of property to the state in consequence of the lack of any individual competent to inherit it.

Estate: This term refers to all the property owned by a decedent at his death and which passes either by his will or by the laws of intestacy. The estate for death tax purposes is not necessarily the same as for administration purposes. The value of many assets may be subject to death taxation through the assets are not subject to administration.

Estate Taxes: Taxes assessed by states and the federal government upon the decedent's right to transfer property. A succession, legacy, or inheritance tax is a tax upon the right to receive property.

Executor/Executrix. A person appointed by a testator to carry out the directions and requests in his will and to dispose of the property according to his testamentary provisions after his decease.

Fiduciary: The term is derived from the Roman law, and, as a noun, means a person holding the character of a trustee, or the trust and confidence involved in it and the scrupulous good faith and candor, which it requires. A person having a duty to act primarily for the benefit of another in matters connected with the underlining. It is something in the nature of a trust, having the characteristics of a trust, analogous to a trust, relating to or founded upon a trust or confidence.

Gift: A voluntary transfer of personal property without consideration.

Guardian: *A* guardian is a person lawfully invested with power and charged with the duty of taking care of the care of the person and managing the property and rights of another person, who, for some peculiarity of status or defect of age, understanding or self-control is considered incapable of administering his own affairs. One who legally has the care and management of the person or the estate, or both, of a child during its minority?

Guardian Ad Litem: A person appointed by a court to look after the interests of an infant whose property is involved in litigation.

Heirs: Historically this had reference to those who took title to an interstate's real property by descent. Many state statutes now define the word to include those persons who take both real and personal property of the Intestate. A living person has no heirs but only heirs apparent.

Holographic Will: A testamentary ardent entirely written, dated, and signed by the testator in his own hand writing: In some states, by statute, based m the Uniform Probate Code, it is only required that the signature and material provisions of the will be in the testator's handwriting

Inheritance Taxes: Taxes assessed on the recipient of the assets and based on the right to receive a decedent; property

Inter Vivos: Between the living; from one living person to another; gifts during one's lifetime.

Intestacy: The state or condition of a person dying without having made a valid will or without having disposed by will a part of his property.

Intestate: Without making a will. A person is said to die intestate when he dies without making a will or dies without leaving anything to testify what his wishes were with respect to the disposal of his property after his death.

Irrevocable: That which cannot be revoked or recalled.

Legacies: Gifts of property, under a will.

Legatee: One who receives property under a will.

Letters Testamentary: The formal instrument of authority and appointment given to an executor by the proper court upon the admission of the will to probate, empowering him to enter upon the discharges of his office as executor

Passage of Title Under a Will: Title to real property passes directly to the devisee, subject to the claims of testator's creditors, but the personal representative has the right of possession during administration. Title and possession of personal property pass to the personal representative and only upon distribution of the estate does the legatee receive title and possession.

Per Stripes (by the stalk. According to the roots, or by right of representation, the issue of deceased children will take their deceased parent's share by right of representation. That mode of reckoning the rights or liabilities of descendants in which the children of any one descendant have to take only the share, which their parents would have taken if alive. For example, suppose a decedent had three children: Jim, Jane, and John, who, if living, would get one third each. If John predeceased the decedent and left ten children, the estate would be divided into twelve equal shares if per capita. If per stripes, the estate would be one-third to Jane, one-third to Jim, and the remaining one-third divided among John's ten children.

Probate: This word describes the presenting of a will to the appropriate court to establish its validity and he entering of the court's order finding that the instrument is decedent's will and admitting it to probate. There follows, as in intestate estates, a process of admiration, the collection and preservation of the decedent's property to those entitled to it by his will or by the statute of descent and distribution.

Probate Court: The court that has jurisdiction with respect to wills and intestacies and sometimes guardianships. Also called surrogates court and orphan's court in some states.

Probate of Will: Formal probate of before the proper officer or court that the instrument offered is the last will of the decedent.

Remainderman: The person who receives property remaining after the death of the person who received the original life interest.

Residuary Clause: The clause in a will, which specifies the disposition of all that is left after indebtedness and bequests, or gifts, are paid.

Residuary Estate: That which remains after the debts and expenses of administration, legacies, and devises have been satisfied.

Revocation of Will. The recalling, annulling, or rendering inoperative of an existing will by some subsequent act of the testator which may be the making of a new will inconsistent with the terms of the first or by destroying the old will or by disposing of the property to which it related or otherwise.

Settlor. The grantor or donor in a deed of settlement. Also one who creates a trust or furnishes the consideration for the creation of a trust.

Specific Legacy: A gift by will of a specific article or a particular part of the testator's estate which is identified and distinguished from all others of the same nature and which can be satisfied only by the delivery and receipt of the particular given thing.

Statutory Share: That portion of a person's property allowed to the spouse by statute.

Subscribing Witnesses: Those who sign as witnesses to a will.

Surrogate: In American law, the name given in some of the states to the judge or judicial officer who has the administration of probate matters, guardianships, and other such matters. In other states, he is called judge of probate, registrar, judge of the orphan's court, and other title.

Testamentary: The expression of an intent to dispose of property by will.

Testamentary Capacity: The competency to make a will.

Testamentary Guardian: A Guardian named in the decedents will.

Testamentary Power: A person who may make a will.

Testate: Having made and left a valid will.

Testator: A man who has left a will at his death.

Testatrix: A female who he left a will at her death.

Will: An instrument executed by a competent person in the manner prescribed by statute whereby he makes a disposition of his property to take effect on and after his death.

Ten Principles for Becoming Wealthy

Ten Principles for Becoming Wealthy

There is a distinct difference between what is necessary to effectively steward money, finances, and possessions for the Kingdom of God, and managing to go to the wealthy place.

Every Christian, whether they make $15,000 or $1,000,000, is called to dominate money and finances. Dominating money and finances means that an individual controls the money that they have, rather than letting the money or lack of it, control them.

Whereas, in order to go to the wealthy place, not only do you have to learn how to dominate money, you must also understand that wealth is transferred through business, and master the principles related to its transfer.

Over 90% of all wealth is accumulated, transferred, and maintained through business and investments. Therefore, the Christian who is called by God to the wealthy place must learn how to dominate in the areas of business and finance.

This section will addresses some important principles that must be mastered on the road to the wealthy place.

Principle #1

Notes

Wealth comes from God.

1 Chronicles 29:10-12

10 Therefore David blessed the LORD before all
the assembly; and David said: "Blessed are You,
LORD God of Israel, our Father, forever and ever.
11 Yours, O LORD, is the greatness, the power
and the glory, the victory and the majesty; for all
that is in heaven and in earth is Yours; yours is the
kingdom, O LORD, and You are exalted as head
over all.
12 Both **riches** and honor come from You, and
You reign over all. In Your hand is power and
might; in Your hand it is to make great and to
give strength to all. (NIV)

Deuteronomy 8:17-18

17 then you say in your heart, 'My power and the
might of my hand have gained me this wealth.'
18 And you shall remember the LORD your God,
for it is He who gives you power to get wealth,
that He may establish His covenant which He
swore to your fathers, as it is this day. (NKJ)

Deuteronomy 28:11-12

11 And the LORD will grant you plenty of goods,
in the fruit of your body, in the increase of your
livestock, and in the produce of your ground, in
the land of which the LORD swore to your fathers
to give you.
12 The LORD will open to you His good treasure,
the heavens, to give the rain to your land in its
season, and to bless all the work of your hand.
You shall lend to many nations, but you shall not
borrow. (NKJ)

Notes

Principle #1, continued

Deuteronomy 30:9

9 Then the LORD your God will make you most prosperous in all the work of your hands and in the fruit of your womb, the young of your livestock and the crops of your land. The LORD will again delight in you and make you prosperous, just as he delighted in your fathers, (NIV)

Proverbs 10:22

22 The blessing of the LORD brings wealth, and he adds no trouble to it. (NIV)

Ecclesiastes 5:19

19 Moreover, when God gives any man wealth and possessions, and enables him to enjoy them, to accept his lot and be happy in his work—this is a gift of God. (NIV)

Principle #2

Wealth is accumulated, transferred, and maintained through business transactions and activity.

Proverbs 13:22

22 A good man leaves an inheritance to his children's children, but the wealth of the sinner is stored up for the righteous. (NKJ)

Ecclesiastes 2:26

26 To the man who pleases him, God gives wisdom, knowledge and happiness, but to the sinner he gives the task of gathering and storing up wealth to hand it over to the one who pleases God. This too is meaningless, a chasing after the wind. (NIV)

Principle #3

Notes

Wealth transfer in business is directly related to the ability to meet unmet needs or solve life problems for profit.

- Advertising - making businesses known
- Automobile industry-transportation needs
- Clothing industry-clothing needs
- Computer industry-managing information
- Dental-dental needs
- Entertainment-entertainment needs
- Financial and professional industry-financial and professional service needs
- Industry-personal business needs
- Real estate industry-housing and business needs
- Restaurant industry-food needs
- Retail industry-retail needs
- Government-policy and procedures, public services (water, electric, police, garbage, etc.)
- Janitoral industry- cleaning needs
- Medical industry-health needs
- Orthodontic industry-malaligned teeth
- Travel industry-vacation needs
- Transportation industry-transportation needs

Notes

Principle #4

Increasing your management responsibility in a successful business increases your potential for wealth transfer.

Luke 12:48

48 . . . For everyone to whom much is given, from him much will be required; and to whom much has been committed, of him they will ask the more. (NKJ)

Principle #5

Identifying and operating in your God-ordained vocation and life's work increases your potential for wealth transfer.

Ephesians 2:10

10 For we are God's (own) handiwork (His workmanship), recreated in Christ Jesus, (born anew) that we may do those good works which God predestined (planned beforehand) for us (taking paths which He prepared ahead of time), that we should walk in them (living the good life which He prearranged and made ready for us to live). (AMP)

Principle #6

Notes

Performing life's work with wisdom, diligence, excellence, integrity, focus, and passion increases potential for wealth transfer.

Proverbs 8:11-18

11 for wisdom is more precious than rubies, and
nothing you desire can compare with her.
12 I, wisdom, dwell together with prudence; I
possess knowledge and discretion.
13 To fear the LORD is to hate evil; I hate pride
and arrogance, evil behavior and perverse
speech.
14 Counsel and sound judgment are mine; I have
understanding and power.
15 By me kings reign and rulers make laws that
are just;
16 by me princes govern, and all nobles who rule
on earth.
17 I love those who love me, and those who seek
me find me.
18 With me are riches and honor, enduring
wealth and prosperity. (NIV)

Genesis 26:12-14

12 Then Isaac sowed in that land, and reaped in
the same year a hundredfold; and the LORD
blessed him.
13 The man began to prosper, and continued
prospering until he became very prosperous;
14 for he had possessions of flocks and possessions of herds and a great number of servants. So
the Philistines envied him. (NKJ)

Proverbs 10:4

4 Lazy hands make a man poor, but diligent
hands bring wealth. (NIV)

Psalms 128:1-2

1 Blessed are all who fear the LORD, who walk in
his ways.
2 You will eat the fruit of your labor; blessings and
prosperity will be yours. (NIV)

Notes

Principle #7

Money and wealth must be managed wisely to maintain the wealth transfer.

Luke 16:10

10 "He who is faithful in what is least is faithful also in much; and he who is unjust in what is least is unjust also in much." (NKJ)

Principle #8

An excellent team of advisors must be developed in order to accumulate and maintain wealth.

Proverbs 15:22

22 Plans fail for lack of counsel, but with many advisers they succeed. (NIV)

Proverbs 12:15

15 The way of a fool seems right to him, but a wise man listens to advice. (NIV)

Proverbs 19:20

20 Listen to advice and accept instruction, and in the end you will be wise. (NIV)

1. Excellent lawyer
2. Tax attorney
3. Excellent accountant who understands the tax system extremely well
4. Insurance agents
5. Life insurance agents: casualty, property, liability (malpractice), disability
6. Financial planner (if necessary)

Notes

7. Investment advisor
8. Real estate agent
9. Banker
10. Consultants

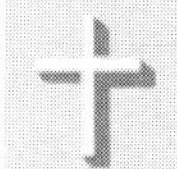

Psalm 1:1-3

1 Blessed is the man who does not walk in the counsel of the wicked or stand in the way of sinners or sit in the seat of mockers.
2 But his delight is in the law of the LORD, and on his law he meditates day and night.
3 He is like a tree planted by streams of water, which yields its fruit in season and whose leaf does not wither. Whatever he does prospers. (NIV)

Proverbs 13:20

20 He who walks with the wise grows wise, but a companion of fools suffers harm. (NIV)

Proverbs 14:7

7 Stay away from a foolish man, for you will not find knowledge on his lips. (NIV)

Be fruit inspectors.

Matthew 7:20

20 Therefore, you will fully recognize them by their fruits. . . (AMP)

1. Are the advisors successful?
2. Who have the advisors helped become successful?
3. Always sift advisors' opinions through the Word of God and prayer.

Notes

Principle #9

Having a generous heart and making others wealthy ensures wealth transfer.

Proverbs 11:25

25 The generous soul will be made rich, and he who waters will also be watered himself. (NKJ)

Proverbs 3:9

9 Honor the LORD with your wealth, with the firstfruits of all your crops; (NIV)

Luke 6:38

38 Give, and it will be given to you: good measure, pressed down, shaken together, and running over will be put into your bosom. For with the same measure that you use, it will be measured back to you." (NKJ)

Psalms 112:5

5 Good will come to him who is generous and lends freely, who conducts his affairs with justice. (NIV)

Principle #10

Trust in God rather than in money and possessions.

Psalm 112:1-3

1 Praise the LORD! Blessed is the man who fears the LORD, who delights greatly in His commandments.
2 His descendants will be mighty on earth; the generation of the upright will be blessed.
3 Wealth and riches will be in his house, and his righteousness endures forever. (NKJ)

1 Timothy 6:17-19

17 Command those who are rich in this present
world not to be arrogant nor to put their hope in
wealth, which is so uncertain, but to put their
hope in God, who richly provides us with everything for our enjoyment.
18 Command them to do good, to be rich in
good deeds, and to be generous and willing to
share.
19 In this way they will lay up treasure for themselves as a firm foundation for the coming age,
so that they may take hold of the life that is truly
life. (NIV)

Notes

Notes

Share Your Personal Testimony With Us

We would love to hear about the awesome things that the Lord has done in your life as a result of your reading and applying the principles we have shared in this book. Let us know how this book has affected you and what other information you would like us to share in future material.

We also invite you to send us your e-mail address, so that we may send you free material on a periodic basis. For more information, visit our web site:

http://www.eaganbooks.com

God bless you!

Remember, God is expecting greatness in your life!

WORKPLACE
WISDOM

Other Resources by
Dr. J. Victor and Catherine B. Eagan

DOMINATING MONEY
Personal Financial Intelligence

- *Dominating Money, 16-Set Series*
- *10 Keys to Dominating Money, 2-Set Series*
- *Eliminating Debt, 2-Set Series*
- *Budgeting, 2-Set Series*

ANOINTED FOR WORK
Using the Tools of Sunday to Succeed on Monday

- *Anointed for Work, 14-Set Series*

DOMINATING BUINESS
How to Prosper on Your Job

- *Dominating Business, 16-Set Series*
- *Servant Leadership, 2-Set Series*
- *What Type of Businessperson Would Jesus Have Been?, 2-Set Series*
- *Your Work Matters to God, 2-Set Series*

HOW TO DETERMINE YOUR MOTIVATIONAL GIFT
Learn How God Wired You

- *How to Determine Your Motivational Gift, 15-Set Series*

HOW TO DISCOVER YOUR PURPOSE IN 10 DAYS
God's Path to a Full and Satisfied Life

- *How to Discover Your Purpose in 10 Days 12-CD Series*
- *How to Discover Your Purpose in 10 Days 12-DVD Series*

HOME-STUDY COURSES available:

- *Dominating Money*
- *Dominating Business*
- *Anointed for Work*

WORKPLACE STUDY MATERIALS:

- *Word @ Work, Volume I*
- *Word @ Work, Volume II*

For more information, visit

www.eaganbooks.com

KINGDOM BUSINESS INSTITUTE

www.kingdombusinessinstitute.com

What is the Kingdom Business Institute?

Kingdom Business Institute is a systematic series of eight, 8-week online courses designed to teach how to practically apply biblical principles and the Word of God in the workplace. The goal is to encourage the character and excellence of Christ in the workplace. Christians should be the most profitable, highly-successful and fully-satisfied people at work.

Who Should Take These Courses?

These courses are recommended for working people, entrepreneurs, business professionals, managers, supervisors and all people in the workplace from the CEO to every level; and anyone called to practice the principles of God in the workplace, namely every Christian.

COURSE OFFERINGS

- HOW TO PROSPER ON YOUR JOB
  Find out what God's Word says about prospering and increasing on your job.
- HOW TO TAKE GOD'S POWER TO YOUR JOB
  Learn how to be more powerful than your non-Christian counterparts.
- HOW TO DETERMINE YOUR MOTIVATIONAL GIFT
  Learn how God wired you and understand why you and others have different views.
- DOMINATING MONEY – PERSONAL FINANCE
  Areas of focus include budgeting, credit, debt, cash flow, estate planning, and more!
- THE CHARACTER OF SUCCESS
  Increase productivity, profitability, and teamwork to excel to the glory of God.
- GODLY LEADERSHIP AND ETHICS
  Integrate highly successful strategies to maximize the gifts and talents of your team.
- DOMINATING MONEY – IN BUSINESS
  Learn how to start and manage businesses and the principles of millionaire thinking.
- HOW TO TERMINATE CONFLICT
  Neutralize conflict completely with superiors, co-workers, and others.

COURSE COMING SOON!!!!
HOW TO DISCOVER YOUR PURPOSE IN 10 DAYS

For on-line course information, please visit
www.kingdombusinessinstitute.com